*Praise for*

# A Magical Course in Tarot

"With a profusion of ebullient, multi-sensory images, Michele Morgan teaches an intuitive, interactive approach to the Tarot that promotes deep engagement with individual cards as well as different types of decks. In this delightful book, Morgan also demonstrates how to discover highly personalized messages through webs of association, the cards' use of body language, the interplay of images, energetic placement, and more."

—Janina Renée, author of *Tarot Spells*, *Tarot: Your Everyday Guide*, and *Tarot for a New Generation*

"I thoroughly enjoyed this book! It's informative, witty, and easy to apply. I applaud Michele for having the courage to make the Tarot her own and teach others how to do that too."

—Nancy Garen, author of *Tarot Made Easy* and *The Tarot According to You*

# A Magical Course in Tarot

## Reading the Cards in a Whole New Way

Michele Morgan

Illustrations by
Rebecca Richards

Conari Press
Berkeley, California

Conari Press, 2550 Ninth Street, Suite 101, Berkeley, CA 94710-2551.

Conari Press books are distributed by Publishers Group West.

ISBN: 1-57324-706-5

Cover photography: © Photodisc
Cover and interior design: Suzanne Albertson
Interior illustrations: Rebecca Richards
Author photo: Terry Reed

*Library of Congress Cataloging-in-Publication Data*

Morgan, Michele.
A magical course in tarot : reading the cards in a whole new way / Michele Morgan.
p. cm.

Includes bibliographical references and index.
ISBN 1-57324-706-5

1. Tarot. I. Title.

BF1879.T2 .M68 2002

133.3'2424—dc21

2001005840

Printed in the United States of America
MG
10 9 8 7 6 5 4 3

This book is dedicated to

Kaeleigh McHenry and Kim Schneider—
two women who changed the shape of my world entirely
and who help me determine each day how I walk in it.

# A Magical Course in Tarot

## part II • Heart and soul



## PART III • Heaven and Earth

# INTRODUCTION

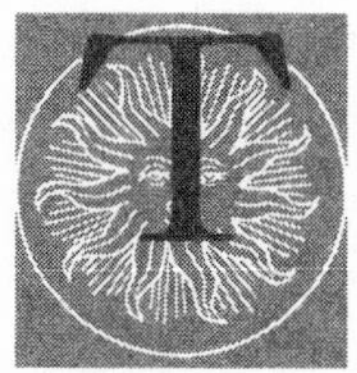

*he Tarot.* The very name suggests mystery, hints at magic, whispers in a language at once universal and arcane. A deck of Tarot cards is an unbound book of spiritual poetry, a visual depiction of life whose symbolism and imagery has remained intact throughout the ages, pure and profound in its wisdom.

Every thought, emotion, deed, or desire in the realm of human experience is illustrated in the Tarot; every possible thread that binds Human and Spirit weaves its magical way through the cards, creating an immediate link to the intuitive voice of our ancestors. No other spiritual tool has such complexity or charm. Whether used for divination, meditation, ritual work, prayer, or healing, or simply to arouse the artistic muse, nothing strikes the soul as deeply and allegorically as the Tarot.

I've been a professional psychic for more than a decade. Tarot cards are my tool of choice; I can access psychic information without them, but the images and their mystery speak to a part of me that no other medium can touch.

I bought my first Tarot deck simply for the pictures. As a writer of fantasy, I'm forever gathering visual treasures to spark imagined landscapes. But something in the cards pulled me in, beyond color and form, to where magical things lay waiting. I attempted to wade through several

"How To" books, seeking access to what appeared secret yet felt as accustomed as my own skin, only to find I couldn't squeeze myself into the structure and form these books demanded. Heavy, encyclopedic, written in serious, scholarly tones, most of the books emphasized study and memorization, and some even directed me to hold the cards a certain way in my hands. I wanted romance and soul; I got rules and regulations, and ultimately, disenchantment.

Then one night in late January, frost on the ground and a mist hazing street lamps and traffic lights, I was drawn to a one-night introductory class at a local metaphysical shop with the divinely befitting name of Stargazers—an enchanted place, filled with crystals by the hundreds, shelves of books, bowls, beads, candles, otherworldly art, and all manner of magical objects, with shimmering sea-green confetti strewn in a trail across the carpet and the sidewalk outside. The Tarot class was being taught by the shop's proprietor, an irrepressible urban goddess with a cloud of dark hair shot with silver, a penchant for amazing jewelry, and a laugh that could be heard in every corner of every room in the store. When I walked into the class that night, the shop warm with candlelight and polished stones, I found myself pulled instantly through the looking glass—but rather than shouting, "Off with her head!," the Queen simply told me to get out of it and get into my instincts instead.

We were shown some of the basics of the Tarot in the first half of the class, such as the symbolic meanings of different imagery, numerology, and color correspondences. Then, in the second half, we were turned loose to read for each other, using nothing but the notes we'd taken in the first half and our raw intuitive senses. I felt as though I'd been given permission to breathe again after a lifetime without oxygen. I tossed my notes and jumped in, heart first, seeing my world for the first time from a wholly magical perspective, and putting into that perspective the intuitive abilities that had shaped and ultimately complicated my whole life up to that moment.

As far back as I can remember, I heard voices. The sound would come as a low, monotone buzzing, like the static of a restless crowd—close enough so that I couldn't ignore it, but far enough so that I could never make out exactly what was being said. I remember straining to comprehend a language, distill even a sentence, a word, anything; sometimes it would paralyze me, this sensation that there was something there I should recognize, something crucial that I alone should know. I was also aware that these voices were not coming from the outside, but rather, from some deep, elemental center of me, and as a result, I remember thinking during these episodes that I must be completely, certifiably crazy.

As we'll be discussing shortly, everyone is psychic; the ability to touch other realms of energy and information is a natural facet of our spiritual beings. For me, this ability came without understanding, in the form of literally "hearing" energy—the collective buzz of the planet and the people around me, translated through my psychic senses, trying desperately to get my attention. There seemed no particular rhythm to when the crowd would show up, but whenever it did, I was compelled to listen, with a mixture of genuine fascination and absolute dread, and with no more understanding of its intention than of its tongue.

What I learned that night in the Tarot class, besides symbology and numbers, was that my ability to "plug in" to the world around me did after all have a rhythm and a purpose—and through the Tarot cards, the energy that had been trying all those years to speak to me finally found its true expression. The looking glass shattered behind me, and there was no turning back . . . and from that moment on, the crowd was thankfully, blessedly silent.

This book began that night, with the consent of a goddess to trust my intuition. The ecstatic discovery of my own true voice became a passion to help others find theirs. I began reading the cards professionally, and eventually I started to teach; my first love coupled with my second brought me to write the kind of book I would have loved to have read when I first began exploring the Tarot—a journal of experience, of sensation, of pilgrimage to magical places; where the cage of tradition and formula is unlocked, dismantled, and left behind as a kind of monument, ivy and morning glory twined all around, honored but ultimately outgrown; a book that gives unadulterated access to the romance and wonder of the cards and absolute permission to trust your own truth, above all else.

You're holding that book in your hands. Here you'll find an exploration of the ancient art of reading Tarot cards, written with magic in mind, rather than science; where rules and tradition indeed have their place, but where instinct and imagination get to roam the woods and play in the meadows first, far from the confines of castle walls.

*A Magical Course in Tarot* is organized into three parts: Part I sets the stage for reading the cards and turning your intuition loose; Part II explores the traditional meanings of the cards, written with a creative twist and enhanced by Rebecca Richards' enchanting and original illustrations; Part II offers other horizons to wander over, such as ritual work and spiritual exploration, and a more in-depth look at the interaction between the cards.

Those of you new to the Tarot, perhaps daunted by the idea of traversing textbooks, memorizing meanings and "doing it the right way," will find my methods delightfully freeing. And those of you who are old hands at this, who know every card by rote, will be liberated and challenged to stretch your intuitive wings and discover new ways to utilize what you know. You can use this book with any Tarot deck; the interpretations of the cards and the accompanying illustrations dance with traditional symbolism, rather than conform to it, offering magical inroads and secret back doors to the heart and soul of the Tarot's timeless wisdom.

A note regarding the spiritual content of this book: You'll find the word *God*, as well as masculine pronouns, used as the primary reference for Spirit. Over the years in my career as a psychic and spiritual counselor, I've found the term "God" to be the easiest to use, since it's the most readily identifiable moniker for Divinity. However, my use of the word is all-inclusive, referencing God, Goddess, Buddha, the All, the Tooth Fairy, and anyone else you happen to believe in. In my "religion," the gods couldn't care less what you call them, as long as you do, so feel free to substitute whatever name you're most comfortable with, and make that association entirely your own.

The Tarot has been called "the royal road to enlightenment." Exploring your own unique connection to Spirit through this mysterious and sacred channel is what this book is all about. May these pages serve as a guide, the cards, as your champion, your own intuitive voice your muse, and this, the start of your journey. . . .

# PART I

# Flesh and Bone

ONE

# The Voice, and a Deck of Cards

## Using the Tarot to Access Intuition

What is the intuitive voice? How do you learn to listen, to distinguish it from all the other voices that clamor and contest for your attention? The voices of intellect and ego; of reason and ridicule; how do you still your mind and allow the whisper of your instinctual nature to rise and be heard above the din?

We live in a world of noise. Where our ancestors once awakened to the cock's crow and the rush of the wind through the trees, most of us come up out of bed each day by electronic buzz or hyper-caffeinated morning DJs. Nights of wolves and cricket song have long been replaced by late-night talk shows and discordant neighbors; we meditate with earplugs, attempt yoga poses tangled in the wires of headphones, and sleep to digital recordings of ancient oceans, trying to conjure sanctuary.

And the hours between waking and sleeping? Traffic, computers, ringing phones, low-flying aircraft, construction sites, twenty-four-hour cartoon networks—feel free to add your own favorites to the nearly endless list. And these are just the *auditory* confusions and stimuli of modern life. The greatest cacophony of all occurs within the coliseum of the human mind, and these musicians never sleep, not even when the ocean you hear from your bedside is real.

Jungian-influenced therapies and archetypal systems have their labels for these rabble rousers—the Wounded Child, the Shadow, the Inner Critic, etc. It is with the input of these very human voices that most of us create our lives. We follow their lead into unhealthy relationships and soul-starved professions, stay at their bidding despite our own misery, and stand shoulder to shoulder with them as they wage war on us regarding the very decisions they helped us to make. I call them The Committee. They gather in a pack, circling, saying Black when you say White, and to distinguish your own truth from theirs, let alone get them to be still, often seems a feat on par with finding the Holy Grail.

Intuition is a voice that resides separate from these. Scientists have divided the brain very neatly into two "hemispheres": the left, wielding logic and rational thinking; the right, ruling creativity and instinct. Intuition lies somewhere between, snuggling with the pineal gland, considered the center of faith in the body. It is the whisper of the gods, conveying its messages via the solar plexus, strung between faith and personal power like tin cans tied to a string. This nearly silent relay of information and energy, from the Third Eye to the third chakra, is what creates the "gut feeling"—the layperson's term for a psychic hit.

## That Little Voice Inside

You know the feeling. That stirring, just below your rib cage, that tells of something beyond what is presenting itself in the moment; something deeper, asking to be known. Sometimes it's a warning, sometimes, a longing; as simple as knowing who's calling before you pick up the phone, as complex as recognizing faces or landscapes that in reality you have yet to see.

Think back to those moments when something inside *just told you to* and you acted. Turning left instead of right at the end of an unfamiliar street, and finding the perfect little rental house with a view of the lake and a landlord who loves cats. Avoiding the macaroni salad at great-aunt Margaret's eightieth birthday party (despite your mother's insistence that second-cousin Missy would be mortally offended if you didn't at least take a bite) and finding out days later that everyone else at the celebration ended up in the local emergency room that night with food poisoning.

Now, think back to the times when you heard that same quiet, unassuming voice, and you *didn't* follow it. Ka-*boom!* Or, at the very least, *Ouch!* Those dead-end relationships and careers mentioned earlier? If reflected upon honestly, there was always a moment before, one solitary heartbeat when you knew, just knew, that you were in for it.

Fight or flight is the primordial reflex kin to intuition; moments of serendipity and luck are its offspring. Trusted, practiced, *believed in,* that feeling of knowing will eventually morph into words and pictures, and you'll have a full-blown psychic experience.

So what is the difference between intuition and psychic energy? In my world, they are one and the same, separated only by degrees, and I tend to interchange the words at whim. Here, for the sake of definition, I will say intuition is the more ethereal of the two: wilder, perhaps, and less defined; more feminine in energy, the yin to psychic's yang. Think faeries in a woodland glade, fluttering in and out of the shadows, wanting you to follow them into the trees but not necessarily willing to draw you a map.

Psychic, on the other hand, is Merlin—propelling Arthur through the forest, opening portals in the sides of rocks, and otherwise offering up the Mysteries of his own volition. Psychic energy is no more tame than intuition, but it is channeled and more focused; the master to intuition's yearling nature. The moral of this story? You have to believe in faeries for awhile, before you can apprentice to Merlin.

On a practical note, the term *intuitive* seems to be more politically correct—and somehow easier for other people to accept—while the word *psychic* carries a distinctly dark and theatrical flair. This sense of drama around all things psychic might explain the popularity and proliferation of 1-900 Psychic Hotlines. Not to invalidate these kinds of services, just the hype surrounding them and the sideshow image that ensues—something I've sought to dispel every day of my career. No gypsy caravans or belly jewels here! (At least none that belong to this lifetime.)

I've known excellent psychics who worked for 1-900 services, and I've also had clients who were robbed blind by them. As in any profession, there are artisans, and there are snake oil peddlers—the responsibility for choosing a valid psychic ultimately lies in the lap of the seeker.

(More on how to choose a psychic in chapter 14.) My biggest complaint with any of the spiritual or occult practitioners out there is the perpetuation of negative and discrediting stereotypes. As a result of the perceptual discrepancies and the existing clichés, there are times when I am careful to describe myself as a professional intuitive, and others, when I fly the psychic flag unabashedly. How do I discern which is appropriate? Why, I follow the faeries into the woods, of course....

Everyone is intuitive. Everyone can master psychic ability. It is not some rare gift, imparted to a select few; it is a spiritual muscle, part of the framework of the conscious human. To say that one person is more intuitive than another is akin to saying one person is more spiritual than another. We are all spiritual; the question is whether or not we choose to develop and express our spiritual natures, of which intuition is principal.

Intuitive information makes itself available in a variety of ways. Just as there are five physical senses to the human experience, so too are there five "channels" of psychic or intuitive input: seeing pictures or images, sometimes known as *clairvoyance;* (2) hearing sounds or words, sometimes known as *clairaudience;* (3) energy sensitivity, sometimes known as *empathic* ability; even through (4 and 5) a psychosomatic experience of taste and smell perceived beyond physical reality. These "Astral Senses," as termed by occultists, operate not through the normal external stimuli, but are connected to and accessed by the state of *knowing* that rises up within us via the intuitive pathway. Some people are more inclined toward a particular sense; others receive information from several, or from all five.

These inner senses unfurl like antennae and reach out beyond our physical and emotional bodies, probing other planes of energy and existence. These other realms are often referred to by specific names, such as the *superconscious,* the *etheric plane,* or the *fourth dimension.* I think of them all as a great big energy stream, pouring along just above our heads, with the collective voice of every soul that has ever existed chattering away inside. The point of strengthening your intuitive/psychic muscle is to be able to dip into this stream at will, consciously focus on a certain voice or voices, and access the most pertinent information for whatever your need.

Much has been written regarding the science of developing psychic ability, the necessity for tools such as meditation and breathing, and the purposeful practice of reaching "alpha" state, where brain wave frequency slows to between seven and fourteen cycles per second, in order to access the higher levels of consciousness. I believe in the importance of any practice that carries us into spiritual silence, and I agree that in order to cultivate intuition, it pays to have good garden tools. However, I also believe there is a distinct difference between science and spirituality, and sometimes the mechanics of science get in the way of the magic of experience. Intuition is much like desire, which requires more faith and faerie dust than physics to materialize. Don't get me wrong—science has its place. But in this particular forest, enchantment is the path to Merlin's door.

## It's All in the Cards

Enter the Tarot, a centuries-old mystical tool for connection and communication with the Divine. Comprised of seventy-eight cards, each one with a specific and profound message, the Tarot speaks in an ancient and evocative language of symbols, charting the evolution of the soul and the mysteries of life. This system of archetypal and emotional imagery makes the Tarot an unprecedented vehicle for spiritual inquiry and intuitive growth.

The mind relates through words and images; the heart, through feelings; the soul, through an innate sense of connection to our God-self. The Tarot links all three by way of universal symbolism, creating a doorway through which the intuitive senses are set free to explore, gather, and translate timeless spiritual wisdom.

The origins of the Tarot are as mysterious as the cards themselves. Stories circulate of ancient Egyptian, Hebrew, and Hindu beginnings; hand-painted cards, circa 1500, from Germany, France, and Italy still survive. It has been speculated that Tarot began first as gaming cards, then became a tool for Gypsy fortune telling; still others believe the cards were used by monks as a means of recording and preserving ancient texts. This cryptic history only adds to the Tarot's appeal. That no one knows the true genesis of the cards, yet all can understand their language, is Spirit at its magical best.

When I hold a deck in my hands, I am reminded, always with wonder, that thousands of other hearts and souls have crossed through this same doorway, transcending time, religion, and the mercurial nature of the human condition to come to a common place, seeking answers from God. And my poet's soul imagines the many hands that have turned the cards and how the questions those hearts have asked are likely not so different from mine.

Buddhists believe the way to enlightenment is through the silence. The Tarot is a remarkable tool for just such a quieting; steeped in symbology and myth, tangible, deliciously visual, it reaches far beyond our modern world, circumventing critics and shadows, carrying us back to a time before alarm clocks and traffic when God sang us awake through the trees.

In the following chapters, we're going to talk Tarot—prospect its symbolism, unearth its secrets, bandy about the rules and traditions, and break most of them in the process—and connect you to your own instinctual wisdom in a way that you've never been connected before. The Tarot is a gateway to Spirit, and while some define intuition as a sixth sense, the Tarot takes it beyond sense to an *essence*—the true voice of the soul.

Are you ready to plug in?

# TWO

# An Owner's Manual

## Choosing, Keeping, and Caring for Your Deck

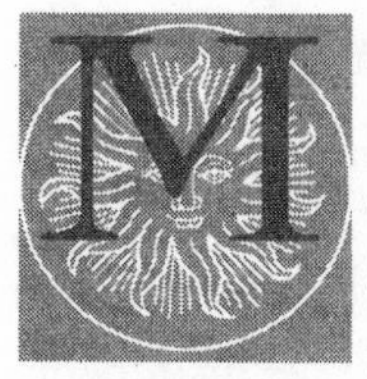

Modern-day playing cards—kin to the Tarot? Some sources say Yes, and the Tarot came first; others say the opposite. One story has the two decks evolving independently of one another and then later converging. What's certain is, not unlike other "relations," there are similarities between playing cards and Tarot cards, and there are differences.

Like its contemporary counterpart, the Tarot deck contains the Ace through Ten of four different suits, as well as corresponding Court cards. The suits in Tarot are traditionally known as Cups, Wands, Pentacles, and Swords, which parallel the Hearts, Clubs, Diamonds, and Spades of a playing deck. And while playing cards have a Court of three, Tarot goes one better with a King, Queen, Prince (or Knight), and Princess (or Page) in each royal house.

These fifty-six cards, known as the *pip* cards of the Minor Arcana, take a slight back seat to the twenty-two *trump* cards (from the Latin *triumph*) known as the Major Arcana, whose messages are always of the highest order. The Minor Arcana represents earthly experience and every manner of human design; the Major Arcana, with such heady characters as the Magician, the Empress, the Lovers, and the Hanged Man, depicts the journey of the spiritual archetype, from innocence to completion, and everywhere in between. The Latin word *Arcana* translates to "Life Secrets." Is that *delicious?* We'll dish the specific symbology of the two Arcanas in chapter 6, but for now, let's go shopping!

## choosing a Deck

There are literally hundreds of different Tarot decks in print. And while most bookstores and specialty shops carry just a fraction of that, it can still seem an overwhelming task to pick from twenty or thirty different selections. So, how do you choose? Some sources will tell you never to buy a deck, that it must be given to you. Still others say, buy your deck and never accept one as a gift. I say, choose a deck that *turns you on.* A Tarot deck should incite your imagination and make you sigh. . . .

There are some definite aspects to consider. First and foremost, how does the deck make you feel? Do the colors engage you? Is the mood of the imagery dark or lighthearted? Do you want a deck with a medieval feel or something more contemporary? Are you looking for a particular mythology, such as Native American, Celtic, or Greek? And what of the medium the artist has chosen—watercolor, fabric collage, pen and ink, or computer-enhanced images?

*Aaargh!* Too many things to think about, you say? I say, *Relax*. This is not really a "thinking" thing. Finding a Tarot deck is much like finding a friend; you begin with an idea of the attributes you're looking for, then trust in the connection when you meet. Besides, here is the perfect opportunity to practice the art of listening to your intuitive voice. More times than not, I have seen someone come into a store with a very particular deck in mind, only to leave with something quite different in hand, and more understanding of magic afoot.

Here's my favorite scenario. Make it a game. Go shopping for a deck on a day when you can spend some quality browsing time. Choose your favorite metaphysical shop or bookstore, or even plan on visiting more than one to compare the inventory. Before you walk in the door, ask your spirit guides, angels, or whomever you believe in to assist you in making the perfect selection. Ask them to make it obvious! Watch for things like one deck upside down on the shelf, when all the others are right side up; a Tarot deck mysteriously tucked in between *Gardening for Beginners* and *The A to Z of Furniture Repair;* a salesperson bringing brand-new inventory out to the floor, and your deck is first on the stack.

This can be tremendous fun, but with a warning: Watch out for falling decks! Literally—my first deck came to me when I went into a B. Dalton bookstore (this was before I realized there were actually "metaphysical" bookstores in the world) armed with intense desire and some extra holiday money. I asked my guides to "make it obvious," and as I was perusing the selection of decks at eye level (I'm only 5-foot-2), from the top shelf high above me, for absolutely no reason other than magical, *The Enchanted Tarot* by Amy Zerner and Monte Farber toppled from its perch and whacked me on the head. Now, this is a deck and book set, mind you, so we are talking about a pretty good whack. Needless to say, I went home with that deck, and a second, tamer selection of my own choosing, a bump on my head, and a new appreciation for spiritual intervention.

If you're not grabbed by a deck right away, don't fret. You will be. Just start looking, being open to messages from your instinctual self. Remember, pay attention to how the deck makes you feel, what emotions the imagery conjures. Color plays an important role, both psychologically and symbolically (more about this and other elements of symbolism in chapter 6), and the more action depicted in the artwork, the better.

Let me clarify *action.* Some decks represent the Ace through Ten of each suit with much the same imagery you would find on playing cards: the Three of Pentacles shows three coins; the Two of Swords, crossed blades; the Ten of Cups has ten chalices in formation. Beautiful? Sometimes. Limited? Always. I recommend you go with a deck that instead offers "scenes": pictures that describe a card's particular energy; lots of people, animals, movement, detail. The key here is to *feel* the cards; I find it much easier to connect emotionally to three people engaged in a horse trade than to three coins on a cream-colored background.

For this reason, it's vital to see the individual cards, rather than just looking at the outside of the box. I have several decks that I purchased by virtue of the box alone (a gorgeous, white-winged angel of Temperance; a serene and dark-eyed High Priestess beckoning from the cover), only to be mightily disappointed when I got them home and saw the complete set. What's that saying, about not judging a book...?!

Most stores offer a sampling of cards from each deck they carry or have demo decks available—opened decks that you can look at and get a feel for in your hands. The hands-on thing is important; *The Voyager Tarot* by James Wanless, which is my primary "professional" deck, is so big that my hands ached for a week when I first started using it! I love it now, but it definitely took some getting used to. How a deck fits and feels in your grasp can be a decisive element in your final choice.

And what if you're given a deck as a gift? The same guidelines apply. How does the deck affect you? What of the color, the artwork, the attitude? Consider the source—is this someone whose energy appeals to you? Is the bestower of the gift a strong and positive influence for you or a benign and neutral one? (Notice I'm not even going into whether they are a negative influence.) If the deck delights you, then thank Spirit and your benefactor and have fun! If not, be gracious and accepting, then either keep the deck for the sake of collecting, or let it journey on to someone for whom it might be better suited. (This is another magical law you can implicitly trust: Spiritual tools always end up in the hands of those for whom they are best intended.)

The bottom line, as always, relies on your intuitive voice. Does the deck feel like it belongs with you? Can you imagine it, years from now, edges worn and colors mellowed, humming in your hands with collected secrets? A Tarot deck should make you feel as if you've just stepped through a doorway and come home.

At the time of this writing, I personally own thirty-eight different decks, and counting. I encourage you to become a collector, to sharpen your intuitive eye with more than one set of images. It's easy when you're first learning Tarot to become very comfortable with a single deck (translation: safe, secure, *stuck*) and after awhile find yourself mentally trapped in the same interpretations for each card, regardless of the question. Multiple decks stretch that comfort zone, keeping your intellect slightly off-balance, which can help you step past your brain and connect with your instinct. Besides, it's creatively enticing to have so much different imagery around to play with.

I liken my decks to four-leggeds or faerie-folk. I have found over the years that each deck embodies a distinct personality, and treated with love, respect, and the reverence they deserve, most have become good friends. The following five decks have grown to be my family.

*The Voyager Tarot*, by James Wanless, made up of sprawling, complex photo collages, is my Industrial Strength deck. For me this deck has a predominant masculine energy; strong, sensual, visually ripped (that's weightlifter jargon for extremely muscular), noble and unflinchingly honest. Picture Hercules, or Mr. Clean, or the huge black Friesian stallion in the movie *Ladyhawke*

I call this one my "No bulls—" deck. When I want the truth, the whole truth, and nothing but, I want the Voyager. The Voyager is the one deck I use with clients, not only for its attitude, but because it's proven to be a never-ending source of fresh information. (Lots of amazing past-life dialogues happen with these cards.) I've used this deck for over seven years now, and I still find that new images continue to leap to my attention. Because the Voyager is so avant-garde, many Tarot beginners feel intimidated by it. Don't be. Its size can take a bit of getting used to, but this deck will make your mouth water. And at the very least, you can be sure you won't get stuck in traditional textbook definitions with these cards.

Now, to the opposite end of the spectrum—the *Hanson-Roberts Tarot.* My wee forest-faerie deck. If I'm in a playful mood, or I'm feeling vulnerable, bruised, and want my answers hummed rather than shouted, you'll find these cards nestled in my hand. Think foxgloves and toadstools; Tinkerbell; the magical white rat who became Cinderella's footman. Sweetest little deck you'll ever find. Traditional in imagery, the drawings are divine, the colors soft, the emotions of the characters worthy of close and frequent contemplation. Amazing how much symbolism is packed into such a small palette! In fact, its compact size and gentle energy make the *Hanson-Roberts Tarot* a perfect first deck for a child or teenager. Angels and appleseeds, inchworms on the morning glories and fireflies on a summer night. Pure enchantment!

And speaking of enchantment ... look at the gorgeous, impossibly intricate fabric collages that compose Amy Zerner and Monte Farber's *Enchanted Tarot.* As recounted earlier, this deck literally fell into my life, and I, for it—romantic, sweeping, once-upon-a-time imagery, colors and textures you'll swear you can *feel;* this deck is the court of Louis XIV, all pomp and circumstance and silk brocade. *The Enchanted Tarot* reminds me of a fairy-tale empress: a strong, wise, gallant woman who can slay a dragon with as much panache as she dances a waltz. I use this deck when I'm feeling majestic; when I'm in the mood for a storybook inquisition; when I want to imagine I'm walking the hallways of a great marble palace, the walls lined with tapestries that recount the collected myths of humankind; when I want to hear the whisper of velvet against my skin, and feel the cool of pearl-stitched slippers upon my feet.

Now, the deck that holds court in all my rituals and spells, has a permanent home on my prayer altar, provides unfailing yet poetic insight into both the mundane and the significant in my life, and is my most intimate and beloved deck is the *Robin Wood Tarot*. A masterful blend of both male and female energy, for me, this deck *is* the Lord and Lady of Magick.

These cards send me, literally—the artwork is so detailed, so rich in color and scope it feels nearly three-dimensional. Regal, sumptuous, a sensory delight; the costumes and faces are from Shakespeare, the landscapes, from Camelot, Avalon, and the forests of Sherwood.

Arthur and Guenevere, Robin and Marion, Herne, Merlin, and Morgan Le Fay . . . the spirits that inhabit this deck are bewitching indeed. When I want to truly experience the myth and magic of Tarot, the *Robin Wood* deck is my key to every kingdom.

The fifth deck in my family is the *Morgan-Greer Tarot*. Color is the driving force for me when it comes to this deck. Moody. Intense. Saturated color. Reds that spill from blood to just-this-side-of-black, summer-twilight greens and *purple*. Not just any purple, either—this is slow-cooked boysenberry jam, African-amethyst, homecoming-confetti *royal* purple. Absolutely delicious. (I used to drive a Geo Tracker named Zoey. Guess what color?)

The imagery of the *Morgan-Greer Tarot* is also striking. Strong faces, plenty of action, stories drawn with wide brush strokes of energy.

A bit more yang than yin, to my eyes; somber and smoky at times; in fact, when I first saw this deck, I thought, Way too dark, definitely not for me. About a year later I saw it again and absolutely *had* to have it! Another reason to collect multiple decks—as you evolve, so will your tastes and interests, and your decks will chronicle that journey.

Some of the other decks that make up my extended family include: the *Aquarian Tarot* (reminds me of the great, stylized "op-art" posters of the '70s); the whimsical *Tarot of a Moon Garden* (think The Beatles' "Yellow Submarine"); the *Gendron Tarot* by Melanie Gendron (dreamy collage-work, lots of animals, fabulous color); *Legend: The Arthurian Tarot* by Anna-Marie Ferguson (stunning watercolor artwork with one of the most amazing bodies of research I've ever encountered—every single card corresponds to a specific aspect of the King Arthur myth. Extraordinary!); the *Universal Waite Tarot* by Mary Hanson-Roberts (a softer, gentler version of the traditional *Rider-Waite* deck); and one of my latest acquisitions, the *Spiral Tarot* by Kay Steventon (action and expression par excellence!).

These are but a sampling, and seen through my eyes. There are unlimited experiences ahead for you if you have the heart and the soul of an explorer.

A word to "beginners"—there are many books, and as many Tarot experts, who will tell you that the only deck you should use when first starting out is the *Rider-Waite Tarot* deck. According to these sources, Rider-Waite *is* the Beginner's Deck. Nothing against the experts or the *Rider-Waite Tarot,* but, *nonsense.* The Rider-Waite is a fine deck, but its imagery is quite formal, and the coloration feels restricted and way too primary for my taste. If the Rider-Waite works for you, great! But don't feel it's a must-have, or that you should start with it first before "graduating" to another deck. Your first, third, or twenty-third deck should come to you by way of your own emotion, desire, and warmth-in-the-belly, instinctual *choice.* Trust it.

## Keeping Your Deck

Alright. So now you've found your chosen deck. The grand adventure has begun. You spirit it home and wait until you're alone in the sanctuary of your favorite room, the music of Clannad drifting from the stereo speakers, spiced candles smoking the air. Breathless, anticipatory, you murmur ancient words of enchantment as you open the miniature chest carved of oak with tiny brass fittings, unfold a scarf of lilac brocade stitched with thin glass beads, and lift the gilt-dusted cards from their sacred sleep. . . .

Okay, so I digress. It will probably go more like this: You carry the deck home in a paper bag, negotiating traffic, two or three cell calls, and a quick stop at the ATM. You feed the cat, check the mail, *then* sit down at the dining room table to savor the moment, sliding the flap free from the cardboard box and peeling the plastic wrapper from the perfect, machine-packaged stack.

Sigh. Well, I still guarantee enchantment, even after cat food and traffic. And once you've disposed of the initial cardboard and plastic, you can employ the miniature oak chest and lilac scarf to keep your deck safe and its energy protected.

It is important to house your deck in something other than its factory packaging. According to some sources, you must use only silk to wrap your deck, because of the vibrational qualities of the material. I say, use whatever you like, so long as it has ambience and meaning. I have wonderful hand-stitched suede pouches, one made with much love by a very artistic friend, stained glass boxes, a tiny antique leather purse from Italy, and yes, several silk bags trimmed with beads. I have velvet bags and embroidered bags, and a simple wooden box with scrolled metal fittings that I found at a flea market, on which my brother carved a beautiful medicine shield to match the *Medicine Cards* by Jamie Sams that live inside.

Very likely the store where you find your deck will also carry a selection of bags or boxes to choose from. Keep your eyes open in gift shops, antique stores, and flea markets as well; trade a reading with an artistic friend; hand pick fabric, ribbons, and beads and spend a quiet afternoon creating. Give your deck a home.

## Caring for Your Deck

Your cherished first Tarot deck. Nestled lovingly in a gorgeous tapestry pouch with tiny copper bells knotted at the ends of the drawstrings. It rests in a revered place on your dressing table, beside the potted ivy and your collection of Zuni fetishes; or perhaps you have tucked it away in a special drawer with a sprig of dried lavender, tied with satin ribbon. Excellent.

Now get it out, for crying out loud, and spend some time with it! You two have got to get to know each other!

When I bought my first deck, I was told I needed to sleep with it under my pillow, so the cards could pick up my vibrations. All I could imagine picking up was a bunch of bent cards off the floor behind the headboard in the morning. I was also told by another source that if I did sleep with my deck, I should remove the Devil card first, so as not to pick up *its* vibrations. Sheesh!

We'll get to the Devil card a little later. As for your cards picking up your vibrations, they absolutely will. But I personally don't think sleeping with them is the way to help that happen. Spend some quality *waking* time with them. Use your cards. Study them. *Hold them.* Nothing real complicated. As you get to know your deck, it will get to know you.

I was also told early on that I would need to clear the energy of my deck each time before I used it as a precaution against negative, confused, even evil vibrations that can accumulate in the cards. This was an idea I really balked at. First of all, I believe very strongly in the Wiccan Threefold Law: What you put out comes back threefold. (Personally, I multiply it by ten.) I give no attention to negative energy; therefore, it pays me no mind, either. Since I believe that evil is a choice, it's pretty easy to avoid, and as for confusion—my interpretation of confusion is that it is a spiritual cocoon, keeping us safely "stuck" and out of our own way so that God can sew on our wings.

From the very beginning, my Tarot decks have been blessed, light-filled guides. The thought of constantly having to clear them of all this supposed bad "stuff" they were absorbing seemed not only an incredibly fear-based process to me, but one that very much underestimated the power of good inherent in these spiritual tools. And besides, being a double Sagittarian, I am sometimes prone to skipping the grunt work and getting to the good stuff.

Consequently, I have found that clearing the energy of my decks only when I feel it's absolutely necessary, or better yet, when I want to indulge in the pleasure of one of these mini-rituals, keeps everyone "clean" and happy indeed. There is always a place for ceremony, when it comes to working with the cards—ritual actions set the stage, and the mood, for magic.

## SMUDGING

Smudging is a sublime Native American practice of burning white sage, cedar, and sweetgrass, and using the smoke to purify. You can buy smudge sticks that have the leaves and grasses already together, bound with colored thread, or you can burn the ingredients loose in an abalone shell or shallow, fireproof bowl. Light the smudge to a good flame, then fan the flame *out;* the result will be a curling column of beautiful, spicy white smoke. (Please use extreme caution when smudging—fire is dangerous, even when it's sacred! Cedar, because of its resin, can flare up easily and tends to pop and spit; and the cinders from smoldering sage can travel very far, very fast.)

To clear your Tarot cards by smudging, hold the deck and move it through the smoke in the four directions, first face up, then face down. You can clear each card individually if you want, but I suggest you move that ritual outdoors, unless you want to end up doing a reading for your local fire department, or for the neighbor that calls 911 on your behalf. (Seventy-eight cards, times a continuous billow of smoke—do the math, and imagine the clouds, spilling out of windows and doors.) A little smudge goes a long way, and the energy of it is truly amazing. I use it not only to clear my cards, but to cleanse and lighten every room in my house (in moderation, of course!).

You can also use incense in a pinch, but once you experience the fragrance and the tangible purity created by smudging, you'll likely be hooked on burning sage and sweetgrass forever.

### SALT WATER BATH

This one I save for special occasions. You'll need a bowl of purified water mixed with sea salt, and a soft, clean cloth. Or, if you really want to go the extra mile, find a ritual recipe for Holy Water in your favorite Pagan or Wiccan sourcebook and whip up a batch beforehand. This can be as casual or as complicated as you like. Dampen the cloth in the water, making sure all the excess is squeezed out, and wipe each card individually, front and back. Your cards will have a waxy coating on them, so the water won't damage them, providing the cloth isn't dripping.

This is a great way to clean the smudges and fingerprints that build up on the cards over time and help even an old, worn deck sparkle again; and the sacred energies of the sea salt and water clear the psychic field around your cards quite nicely. This is a great clearing to do on a special day, such as your favorite Sabbat on the Wheel of the Year, or your birthday, or perhaps New Year's Eve.

One year I did this at midnight on the Winter Solstice, candles burning everywhere, wearing my favorite ritual dress and jewelry, with feet bare and hearth blazing. I shuffled the deck I was going to clear and then set it face down on the table in front of me, and before I picked up each card to bathe it, I allowed a question or thought about anyone or anything at all to randomly pop into my head. For more than two hours, I sat in a state of magical astonishment and ecstasy, as each of the seventy-eight cards I turned over made a very exact and insightful statement regarding the "random" thought that proceeded it!

### MOONLIGHT

This one's a personal favorite. Ingredients: your deck, a windowsill, table, or other flat surface, preferably one that can go undisturbed for at least ten hours (translation: out of the path or the reach of the C.A.T) and a glorious, ripe, silver-breasted Goddess of a Full Moon. Wait 'til She's up, dancing on said surface, and set your deck full in Her splendor. I swear, your cards will be glowing in the morning! (Note to the obsessives in the audience: As the Goddess makes Her way across the sky, so Her light will make its way across the table or windowsill. Move your deck accordingly until you go to bed; it isn't a spiritual necessity to awaken every hour to make sure the cards are constantly lit. The Goddess knows what She's doing; moondust spreads, even in shadow.)

### SUNLIGHT

Same as the previous instructions, only with a twelve-hour time difference either way. I personally employ this only when I need a more aggressive cleansing; this is the God, after all, and He is a bit more forceful about these things! I have seen the colors on a deck fade from too zealous an application of this technique, so save this one for once-in-a-while.

### EARTH

This one is a definite extreme. Personally, if I thought a deck needed this kind of cleansing, I'd probably burn it and get a new one. Wrap the deck *carefully,* in several layers of sturdy, natural fiber cloth. Bury it. Some sources say leave it for three days, some say seven. I'm sure there are many other schools of thought. What do I say? Class? *Use your intuition!* However long you want to leave your deck buried, that's how long you leave it. The idea here is to allow the Earth's energy to neutralize and purify the cards. I've never used this technique, due to my previously stated feelings, and also because I live in the Northwest, famous for slugs, moss, and neighborhoods with questionable drainage. Seasonal discretion is advised.

### CRYSTALS

The same energy as the Earth technique, only a lot more practical and a lot less messy. Remove your deck from its bag or box, and set it somewhere it can rest undisturbed for as many days as seems appropriate. Surround the deck with crystals, or simply place one on top. Quartz crystals are perfect, as they generate very powerful healing auras. Here, also, use your instinct; choose crystals that speak to you, are your personal favorites, or have the particular properties of cleansing, healing, neutralizing, etc. Some people advocate always keeping a crystal in the pouch with your deck; I tried this once, loving the idea, but because my decks travel with me so much, the cards became scratched and dented in no time. If you're not planning on making your deck mobile, a companion crystal in its home is a great all-purpose, all-the-time clearing.

## SORTING

I love this method. Simple, easy, requires no extra "stuff," and it's downright hypnotic. Put your cards back in numbered order. That's it. The Major Arcana, zero through twenty-one; the suit cards, Ace through Ten followed by the Court cards in their appropriate hierarchy. Then stack the Major Arcana on top of the four suits, in whatever order feels good to you. You're done! When you reshuffle, you'll feel a difference, a freshness; a bit like taking them out of the cardboard box all over again.

## TAPPING

Lastly, for the quick fix, just take your deck and tap it on the table or the palm of your hand a few times. I use this in the event that I bungle the wording of a question (more on asking questions in chapter 4) or I feel like my focus was scattered and the cards before me just don't make sense. Tap, tap, tap. (Three is one of my magic numbers; please feel free to choose your own!) I picture a scenario somewhat like Pigpen, from the Peanuts cartoon; when he takes a step, the dust falls around him in little gritty clouds. Tap the deck, the static energy falls away, and you're good to go. It's fast, cheap, and for minor matters works like a charm.

And while we're on the subject of clearing energy—I am often asked whether or not you should allow other people to touch your deck. I believe this should be a personal decision. Again, I've seen it written as a never, ever, hard and fast rule; something more about negative, dark energies finding their way into the cards. I am so blessed to have the caliber of clients and friends that surround me, it is a privilege and a pleasure to have them touch and admire my decks. I feel they amplify and spread the magic, rather like butterflies and faerie dust.

I have also heard the opposite directive—you *must* have the "querent" (the person for whom the reading is being done) shuffle and cut the cards, so as to connect the deck with their energy and facilitate the reading. In chapter 4, we'll discuss shuffling in preparation for a reading and so more directly address this issue; once more, let your instincts guide you as to the handling of your own decks. My *Robin Wood* deck, which resides on my altar, I reserve for my own private use; not because I don't want anyone to touch it, but because it has grown so sacred and intimate to me. But definitely don't fear letting others handle your decks—let that decision come from integrity rather than distrust.

Treat your decks as you would a precious spiritual heirloom—a family Bible, your grandmother's rosary, a menorah that once belonged to a dear friend. Keep them private and personal, or let them be shared and treasured, whichever feels right to you, and you'll find they grow more meaningful and even more magical as a result.

## THREE

# Finding Buried Treasure

## Opening to Your Intuition

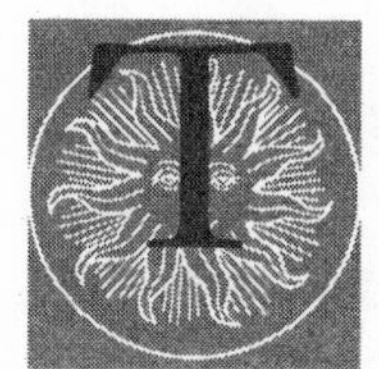

The candles have been lit in their tarnished goblets, the flames throwing scintillas of light over the quiet room, golding the pleats of the curtains drawn at the windows, softening the worn damask of the shawl that drapes the low, round table before you. An empty velvet bag lies near your elbow like the chrysalis of some mythic insect, long since flown away; across the tabletop, a swath of jewel-colored cards spread out in a peacock's fan. And you, cross-legged on the floor, chin in hand, study the tableau with an expression of awe and wonder on your face and one simple question floating before your mind's eye.

*What in the heck do these things mean?*

Ah. Patience, grasshopper. Before we talk meanings, let's talk about where the meanings come from.

The language of the Tarot is timeless and as multilayered as an archaeologist's dig. So much emphasis is placed on the traditional or "book" definitions of the cards, and while they definitely have their place in a good psychic reading, these habitual descriptions are merely one slice of the mystical strata. Let's begin at the deepest, or truest layer, first—your immediate, instinctual *reaction* to the Tarot's imagery.

Have you ever bought a book simply because you were drawn to the cover? Were you ever stopped in midstride by a painting or a photograph glimpsed in a crowded shop window, or compelled to tear out a magazine ad and keep it in a drawer somewhere because it spoke to something inside of you? *That* is the doorway. Your first emotional response, regardless of tradition or definition, is the first step on the path of intuitive discovery.

## first impressions count

Your first intuitive impression, prompted by a card's imagery, might well show up in a flash of crystalline detail—a face you know as well as your own, a history or experience you completely comprehend. Or, it may come simply as a *feeling*—you turn a card, and an undefinable sense of happiness, or sorrow, or regret, lifts its hand to you. *Follow it.* Move lightly, as you would move near a wild creature glimpsed in its natural habitat; a fawn, dappled by sunlight filtering through the trees, or a raven, gliding in silence through a woodland glade. This is not capture and contain; like a dream, these first fleeting energies can disappear like smoke through your fingers if you hold to them too tightly. But if you simply follow the deer through the woods, giving your emotions and impressions room to wander, all manner of symbolism will appear on the path before you, drawn by your receptivity. Colors, patterns of objects, numbers, expressions on the faces of the characters in the cards all will approach you, all with something wild and remarkable to share.

As the psychic landscape continues to expand, the symbols that matter most to your personal mythology will also rise and demand your attention. Like the pages of some grand and ancient atlas will come the lyrics of a song, the thread of a conversation heard weeks ago, and yes, even the traditional meanings of the particular card—all opening to you, all suddenly, magically apropos.

When I was a kid, I used to love treasure hunts. So much so, that for many years my mom would stay up the night before my birthday, feverishly writing clues (rhyming, no less!) on index cards and scraps of colored paper, hiding them all over the house so I could run around the next morning on the trail of something wonderful. Working intuitively with the Tarot has that same feel—enchantment, anticipation, the unexpected twist of being drawn in fresh directions, and the knowledge that you're destined to find treasure.

Emotion. Memory. Experience. Desire. Dream imagery, pop culture icons, classic literature, movie scripts, even bumper stickers spied in rush hour traffic—all these are channels through which Universal wisdom can communicate. The challenge is to gather these myriad languages together and apply them to the question at hand; the magic lies in being open to the clues, following the signposts of your imagination and instinct until the perfect message offers itself up to you and the treasure is found.

Even universal symbolism is open to interpretation. For instance, the image of a cross—ancient, sacred, traversing centuries of religious intent—can mean very different things, depending upon your personal viewpoint. The emotional connection to a particular symbol has some to do with collective iconology, but more to do with how one's own blood runs through their veins. Does this mean you will only receive psychic information through the Tarot that agrees with your personal viewpoint? Absolutely not. It means the images and channels by which that information avails itself to you will be largely determined by your emotional/psychological "fingerprint," and that's what makes the Tarot such a unique and wondrous tool for discovering just what makes you tick.

For example: Take the Three of Wands from the *Robin Wood* deck—three ships on a golden sea, a man standing on the shore, his crimson cloak billowing in a warm wind, a stave in his hand shining like a signal lamp. Working solely from an intuitive stance, you might see the card as the bold anticipation of fortune's arrival. Someone else might see the three ships *leaving* port, carrying that fortune away. The emotional appeal for you in this case would make this card a perfect messenger of approaching opportunity or impending gifts; for the other, a portent of lost chance and silent longing.

But isn't this just as limiting as going by the book meanings? Can't you become equally stuck interpreting images emotionally, based on personal sentiment? That's the magic of following your intuitive impulse. Intuition is not attached to emotion; it's merely inspired by it. When in this moment, you see the ships arriving, in the next reading, you might very well see them sailing away to lands beyond.

Divine Wisdom, your guides, Spirit, God—whomever you choose to connect to, and whatever you choose to call them—in league with your deck, will give you whatever cards are appropriate, at any particular time, in any particular reading, to give you the clearest, most powerful message possible.

Yet another reason to hold off on the traditional meanings of the cards until your intuition has had a chance to comment: Say your first instinctual reaction to the Nine of Wands is a sensation of exhaustion, but you look it up in a book, and find it described as a card of great strength and a warrior's zeal. Hmmm. Confused? Let me bet which definition you'll drop the fastest! Remember The Committee? Well, they're going by the book, I promise you.

Don't get me wrong here. The book definitions of the cards are important and powerful—they are based upon the universal meanings of symbols and archetypes, steeped in tradition and ancient wisdom, part of the timelessness of the Tarot and its language. What I'm saying is, if you limit yourself to using only the book definitions as your means of finding answers, you cheat yourself out of the most magical aspect of working with the cards—priming your intuitive abilities. If you practice following the deer through the woods when you're using the cards, you'll be able to follow that critter anywhere, with or without a deck in your hands—through conversations, experiences, personal transformations and life decisions, and you'll always be led to the truest answer.

If you use book meanings to define the psychic doorway, you're running with your intellect, not your intuition, and the path pretty much stops there. Not to mention the fact that in many books, the definitions can run the gamut from blissful to bleak for a single card, and then you get to spend even more intellectual energy trying to decide which one applies—in the meantime, the deer (and the faeries, for that matter) will have high-tailed it back into the forest.

Here's an example: The Three of Swords can be found defined in books (and sometimes in a *single* book) as everything from successful surgery to grieving over a sudden tragedy. What if you pulled that card for a reading regarding a minor hospital procedure? Which definition do you think you'd choose? And would you be able to choose without doubting the answer?

Or, take the Seven of Cups—known in book definition as chemical dependency, tremendous creative inspiration, and several things in between. (Again, sometimes all in one shot.) If you had recently met someone you were interested in, were inquiring about their character, and pulled that particular card, would you be able to decide between an addict and an artist without questioning yourself? Or them?

If you allow your intuition to speak first, you'll *feel* the relevant definition, then be able to apply the appropriate book meanings to your reading, as well as any other magical tidbits of information that float your way. There's plenty of room for book definitions, but only after your intuition has led you to the one that matters most. I cannot emphasize enough the importance of letting your instincts be your guide, especially at the beginning.

When you're first learning to trail the wild beast through the forest, the last thing you need is to be fumbling in your backpack for someone else's map. Practice following your own definitions for awhile, before you break out the books and start analyzing the terrain. Besides, what would you rather be doing right now with that deck of yours—memorizing meanings or going on a treasure hunt?

## Do Try This at Home!

When I teach Tarot, I use the following exercise to illustrate the often huge discrepancies between intuitive hits and traditional definitions:

Hold your deck so the cards are face up. Spending no more than one or two seconds on each, go through your deck, one card at a time, and separate them into two categories. A "positive" pile, containing the cards whose imagery immediately inspires, uplifts, invokes a sense of peace or joy; and a "negative" pile—the cards that, the moment you see them, either make you merely uncomfortable or absolutely recoil. Don't *think* about your choice; *feel* it. No going back and changing your mind, either! Now, go through each pile again, just as quickly, narrowing the cards down to your five favorites and the five absolute worst.

At this point, grab a book and see if your choices "agree" with the written definitions. Sometimes they're spot on, and sometimes it's amazing to see just how different they are. (This, of course, can also vary depending upon which book you're using—another point of confusion and unnecessary conflict.) Students are dumbfounded when I pick apart their "happy" cards in this exercise, using book definitions as my weapon. The Moon, seen by one as a silvery, enchanting Goddess of intuitive insight, is described in some books as dishonesty, nightmares, and disillusionment. Or the Six of Swords, which appears at this moment as a peaceful voyage, perhaps spiritual in nature, is defined on paper as a journey of loss and defeat.

The negative pile can be just as contradictory. Someone might see the Two of Swords as a card of impasse and uncertainty; certain books define it as peace and tranquility after conflict. Or the Four of Pentacles, which, in the hands of some artists, appears as a conniving, grasping Scrooge, is often defined as wealth and financial security.

I've seen traditionally positive cards such as the Prince of Wands end up in the clinker pile, simply because someone reacted to the particular expression on the Prince's face or the attitude of his fiery horse. And I've also seen that same Prince on the "go" pile, yet described in other books as a rash, untrustworthy, and manipulative rogue. Go figure.

And speaking of that charmed Prince . . . I find the Court cards consistently the most baffling and difficult of the Minor Arcana for my students to interpret, particularly if following the conventional theory held in most books, which is that when a Court card appears, it means a person having those particular traits is involved at the present or will be showing up anytime soon. This is especially confusing if the question being asked isn't "people oriented"! Letting the intuitive nature explore these royal characters allows a much broader picture to be painted, one based on energy rather than exposition.

Again, this is not to imply that the book meanings are incorrect—they are but one layer of symbolic information, and given all the variables of author, artist, and intent, the surest way to connect to the *appropriate* book meaning is by following your intuition out of the gate.

Your first intuitive impulse will also take your eye to individual images contained within the cards that are the most applicable to the given inquiry. With the Ten of Swords, in one reading you'll definitely see the figure pinned to the ground by a gauntlet of blades; in the next, you might instead be drawn to the glow of the sun breaking through the clouds on the dark horizon. The King of Cups may appear for one question as a benevolent mentor, handing you knowledge and creative insight; in another, the chalice he holds may present itself as a symbol of a drinking problem someone close to you is trying to hide.

These dichotomies of definition are made all the more apparent when you work with more than one deck. The same card, even when depicted with similar imagery, in two individual decks can appear dramatically different, simply by way of color, expression, scenery, or rendered mood. By allowing your first reaction to lead the way, you'll uncover any and all pertinent information, whether reeled in from the stream of collective consciousness or gleaned ultimately from the books.

Try this "good card versus bad card" exercise; then try it again a month from now. You'll very likely end up with some of the same cards in each pile but find a number of them have switched sides—just shows you the different energies you're tapping into at any given moment. Rest assured that you will always have favorites, as well as those that make you cringe; rather than being a liability, these cards serve to illustrate the deepest joys and fears you carry within you and, over time, will help chronicle your spiritual growth and evolution.

As for learning the book meanings . . . take your time. I tell my students who are new to the cards not to touch a Tarot book for three months; and those who've already been using the book meanings, to put them away for the same amount of time. Give your psychic muscle a chance to strengthen first before you engage it in an inevitable wrestling match with your intellect. The more you work with the cards, the more connected you will become to them, individually and collectively, and then you can begin to learn their symbolic and historical connotations from a much more objective standpoint. Let that part of the process be a natural one, as well—just as allowing your intuitive senses to rise in you is as natural as watching that deer ambling through the sunlit woods.

## A Few Good Myths

Now, before we move on to the nuts and bolts of an actual reading, I'd like to address a few points of curiosity that inevitably pop up in the process of discovering Tarot, thanks in great part to years of religious and social misrepresentation. I'm not pointing fingers in any particular dogmatic direction—suffice it to say, ignorance is *not* bliss, at least not for those on the receiving end. That said, here are a few records set straight:

### Is the Devil an evil card?

Kind of like asking if a certain rock is evil, or a toothbrush, or a bagel. It all depends upon your belief system. If you believe in the Devil or Satan as an actual entity, then I suppose your first inclination would be to associate the card of the Devil with its namesake. However, the card itself cannot contain any energy other than that which you assign it—and for the most part, even the traditional meanings of the Devil card lean toward the *fear* of evil rather than the actual force itself. Evil is a choice, not an energy, and given that, the Devil card can offer a rich and fascinating panorama of information.

### What about the Death card?

Death is always the card that gets placed on the table in the flickering lamplight by the dark-eyed Gypsy princess, for the theatrical terror of the innocent querent, in all the best murder mysteries and horror novellas. Outside of fiction? In reality, as in nature, Death is the doorway to rebirth. Rarely have I ever picked up physical demise from this card; however, it has definitely signaled the end of relationships, jobs, life phases, and unhealthy behavior patterns. For every ending, there is a beginning . . . that's Cosmic Law.

### Can you manipulate a reading?

That's actually a great question, and I'll be the first to tell you I've certainly tried in my time! Once, very early on in my relationship with the Tarot, I remember asking the same question of ten different decks, getting more and more frustrated that I wasn't "hearing" what I wanted. Not to mention each deck gave me nearly identical cards. (What's that saying, about the definition of insanity? Doing the same thing over and over again, expecting different results?) The only way you can truly manipulate a reading is by doing what I just described, or purposely misinterpreting the cards, either of which will be painfully, and in retrospect, embarrassingly obvious. Coming up, we'll be discussing energy and emotional influence on a reading, and other matters of intent. But if you're truly using the cards as windows to Universal Wisdom, you can only get "right" answers.

**Will I be in danger of contacting "dark" or negative energy working with the cards?**

Another nod to Hollywood. My standard reply to this kind of question is, *Only if you ask for it.* Like vampires—they can only cross the threshold of your home if you invite them in. The Tarot is a sacred instrument of spiritual design; if you do contact dangerous energy while using it, I guarantee you won't have the cards to blame for it. Don't focus on dark or negative things, and they won't throw a party in your living room. Capiche?

# FOUR

# On Your Mark, Get Set. . . .

## Preparing for a Reading

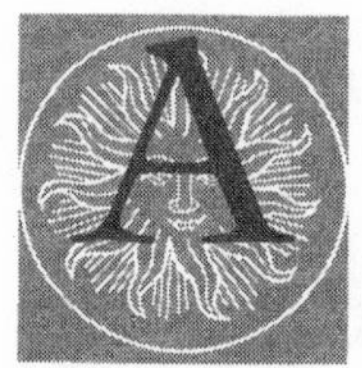

maiden voyage; uncharted terrain. You begin your journey as any intrepid explorer—armed with water skins, compass, and charts, a pouch full of trinkets to trade with friendly natives, a warm cloak, and the stars, mapped out in your mind, the constellations named and familiar as kin. You return from that journey forever changed, gifted, carrying a journal of experience, packets of seeds, the memory of winds, warm and holy, and a calling to go back, to explore the landscape once more with deeper eyes.

And so you venture to that place, again and again, discovering pools of still water to drink from, ancient oaks and rock formations that mark the horizon, and natives who smile and welcome you to their fire as a friend. And even the stars in that magical sky, known as they've been from the beginning, each time offer up new and remarkable designs, expanding the boundaries of your own world with endless possibility.

So it is, exploring the landscape of the Tarot. The unknown will invite you to become a familiar; the familiar will constantly stretch and expand itself and you along with it. In the beginning, your journeying will fare better with some provisions and planning; the more trips you take, the more you can learn to live off the land.

In this chapter, I'm going to offer you the "bones" of a Tarot reading—the essential tools to begin your explorations with courage and comfort. I advocate traveling light, as you'll see. Less equals more, in my experience—more freedom, more self-reliance, more appreciation and connection to the territory around you, and more opportunity to trust the guidance of Spirit. Besides, you'll want room in those saddlebags for bringing home treasure. . . .

## preparatory Ritual

*Ritual* is defined by Webster as "a ceremonial act." Ritual is a mood maker; the simplest deed, done with intent, can transform worldly circumstance into communion with the Divine. Working with the Tarot naturally lends itself to magical actions; the very temperament of the cards sets the stage for ceremony.

Many sources insist upon specific forms of preparatory ritual before doing a reading. I've seen these prescribed practices range from simple breathing exercises to complex combinations of guided visualization, meditation, chakra clearing, and prayer. While it is important to be as calm and connected as possible when you work with the cards, if sitting in a lotus position taking deep, rainbow-colored breaths for ten minutes before picking up your deck doesn't do it for you, here's a chance to find out what does.

Create the rituals that suit you best. It might be that you simply choose a particular place to do readings—a vintage parlor table in the corner of your bedroom, the living room sofa, draped with your grandmother's shawl, or the breakfast nook you transformed into a pillow-lined meditation chamber. A particular time of day might afford you more sanctuary or spiritual ambience than any other. You may find a favorite prayer or song helps to center you and ground your energy. A few slow breaths, a moment or two of stillness, a candid request of the gods for guidance and light—any deliberate action that establishes spiritual intent and shifts your consciousness to the work at hand is ceremonial, no matter how simple or seemingly mundane.

Now, there's no denying the magic of spreading the cards out on a crystal-scattered table in the candlelight, with burning incense and moody music; atmosphere is an essential part of *any* ritual. But just as a prayer reaches heaven whether it's whispered aloud or sung and danced in a sacred circle, the cards are a spiritual tool, and if you view them and treat them as such, simply taking them from their box or bag will serve to connect you.

My favorite Tarot ritual? Depends upon my mood, my environment at the moment, and the purpose of the reading. When I'm at home, with time to spare and a yen for the mystical, candles and crystals are an absolute, usually followed by a cat or two, either on my lap or sprawled across the cards, for that little added touch of witchy magic. At my prayer altar, all I need to do is light the lamps, entreat the gods, and I am instantly transformed. But more often than not, my pre-reading practice consists of picking up a deck and shuffling. That's it. My decks have become such an extension of me that the very act of holding the cards in my hand is a ceremony.

## shuffling

Shuffling the cards grounds me. It's hypnotic. Sometimes I shuffle a deck just for meditation, without even pulling a single card. You're going to find a great many directives regarding this topic in different books; as usual, you have my unadulterated permission to use whatever method works for you. The only hard-and-fast here is to keep the cards face down. Unlike the earlier exercise, where you looked at the cards and their imagery for the purpose of choice, for an actual reading you're going to choose the cards "blind," guided by instinct and Spirit. This helps circumvent matters of will and personal control. And besides, the more mystery and intrigue in a reading, the better!

Shuffling the cards before you lay them out is essential for several reasons: it clears the energy of the deck, gives you an opportunity to concentrate on the question or issue at hand, and mixes up the cards to ensure a clean "pull." (Pulling, or choosing, cards—coming up!)

Depending upon the size and flexibility of your deck, you can employ the ever-popular "arch-and-fan" method of shuffling, an impressive favorite of blackjack dealers everywhere. (I try not to bend my decks too dramatically when I do this. It definitely adds to the mileage of everyday use.) If your chosen deck is too large, or the cards too heavy, you can simply let them "fall"—split the deck in two, make an A-frame with the two piles in your hands, side by side; let the cards fall together, alternating from each side, to form a single pile again. Picture batter being poured into a cake pan, folding back and forth on itself. Or, you can shuffle the deck kid-style—hold the cards in one hand, and drop them in random chunks into the other.

How long should you shuffle the cards before you begin a reading? I've seen instructions that literally count the shuffles, including cutting and restacking the deck *x* number of times; my attitude is to shuffle until you feel like you're finished. (Another great opportunity to dance with the faeries.)

If you're doing a reading for someone else, is it necessary to have that person shuffle the deck? Here, again, I advocate personal choice. Some say it's a must-do, in order to infuse the cards with the querent's energy and ensure a clear reading. If you're working with the cards intuitively, you're tapping in to Universal Wisdom and that can be done with or without physical contact.

I used to have my clients shuffle the cards before their reading, just because; this frequently ended up as an awkward moment, with my client either unsure how to shuffle or fearful of damaging the cards. Finally, the following experience convinced me to stop this optional custom altogether:

A young woman came to me for a reading, obviously troubled and more than a little bit nervous. I handed her the deck, told her to think about her situation, focus her energy, and to shuffle the cards until she felt guided to stop.

It all began innocently enough. She shuffled the cards, very deliberately, with a great expression of concentration on her face. Shuffling. Shuffling. As was my custom, I sat quietly, in a prayerful manner, holding the energy of the moment. Shuffling. Shuffling. Still shuffling. I waited, wanting to honor her process, imagining she must be in a state of profound turmoil and in need of this extra meditation. *Twenty minutes later,* I cleared my throat and asked softly if perhaps she thought the deck might be ready by now. She looked up at me with a mixture of surprise and relief, and replied, "Oh! I was waiting for you to tell me when to stop!"

If having your querent shuffle the cards feels like a powerful and sacred part of your pre-reading ritual, then by all means, hand over that deck! If not, shuffle away in your own inimitable style and don't doubt your ability to connect.

## pulling, or choosing, cards

This is where the magic *really* begins. Choosing the cards for a Tarot reading can turn the most die-hard skeptic into a born-again believer; pretty much impossible to discount mystical influence when you're exploring your relationship and the first card to pop up depicts someone who bears an uncanny resemblance to your mate in question. Or perhaps you're wondering whether or not to move to a warmer clime, and three out of four cards you choose depict sunshine and desert terrain. The fourth? The Chariot, or perhaps one of the Princes, their horse galloping full speed ahead toward a new adventure.

After shuffling the deck to your liking, you can choose the cards for your reading by taking them one by one straight from the top of the deck, or by spreading the entire deck out in a fan and allowing your hands to be guided to particular cards. Sometimes, a card or two may fall from the deck while you're shuffling, and you can be sure you're meant to include those in your reading. (Several of my decks *love* to do this to me, scattering cards every which way—rather like a mischievous toddler tossing his toys to the floor time and again, just to watch Mom keep on picking them up. . . .)

My favorite technique is to let your deck choose the cards for you—a method I call *splitting:* Hold your deck cupped in the palm of one hand. Tip the deck slightly (to the left if the deck is in your right hand, to the right if it's in your left), allowing your hand to slowly open; the cards will slide to the side in chunks, and wherever those "splits" appear, that's the card to pull. This is really fun and carries a tremendous miracle quotient—hard to deny the energy of Spirit when you can watch and feel the cards move, seemingly of their own accord, in your hand.

Whatever method you decide upon, it helps to be consistent, especially in the beginning; your decks will literally get to know you and how you operate, and this helps ensure even more powerful messages through individual cards. I can't emphasize enough here that *you cannot choose an incorrect card.* (More than once I've pulled a card, hesitated, stuck it back in the deck and reshuffled, only to have the same card come *flying* out again, almost indignantly.) You might indeed misinterpret the cards, as we'll be discussing a little later, but no matter how you go about it, whatever you're drawn to pull, or that falls (or leaps!) from the deck, is a card that has a distinct message for you.

## upright versus Reversed cards

Another Tarot tradition worth mentioning and amending: Upright versus reversed cards. According to convention, when a card lands right side up in a reading, it's considered *upright.* The ones that fall upside down are called *reversed.* And yes, this means that when a card is reversed, it has a different meaning than when it appears upright. Daunting enough to have to memorize the definitions of seventy-eight different cards, but *twice* that? Yikes!

There's another school of thought that says if a card falls reversed, rather than having a different meaning, it simply bears a closer look than the cards surrounding it—sort of like it's trying to get your attention by misbehaving.

In my school? There are no reversed cards. Reading the cards intuitively *requires* they be upright, so you can see the images clearly and without interruption—the cards tell a story when you lay them out in front of you, and nothing ruins the rhythm of a good read like turning a page and finding it's been printed upside down! Keep all the cards in your deck upright, all the time. Problem solved.

## phrasing questions

Most of the time when you sit down with the cards, you'll have a particular issue in mind that you're seeking insight into. Other times, you may simply feel restless in your life, or uncertain, and will be looking for a bit of solid ground to stand on. The clearer you can be about *why* you're seeking insight, the clearer and more direct the information will be, particularly when you're first starting out.

Keep your questions as simple as you can, with the emphasis more on experience than outcome. For example, say you have a job interview coming up and want to find out how it will go. Your first inclination will probably be to ask, "Will I get the job?" While this is indeed a simple and straightforward question, it's also limited to a Yes or No answer, setting you up for a whole lot of head tripping about positive and negative cards and hindering the opportunity to gain valuable insight into yourself and the situation.

Instead, asking, "What conditions will I encounter in the job interview next week?" or, "How will next week's interview affect my career?" opens the way for insight into the mood of the interview, the energy of the company, the potential relationship with superiors, and the future of your professional path. Other effective questions are, "What do I need to know in order to do my best in the interview?" "What should I focus on during the interview?" "What challenges, if any, do I need to be aware of?" This last question is particularly powerful in bringing to light (and thus giving you a chance to overcome) any kind of block, either in the situation itself or within you, that might otherwise have preordained the outcome.

These same kinds of questions can be utilized for any situation: relationship, family, health, finances, etc. "What do I need to know about my partner's emotional process right now?" is going to yield far more useful information than "Has Johnny stopped loving me?" Got a new love interest? Try, "How will this relationship progress in the next (few days, weeks, months, etc.)?" as opposed to "Will Prince Charming ask me out again?"

Regarding money issues: "What do I need to know in order to capitalize on my current investments?" works better than "Will my stocks do well in the market?" And, "What is the best course of action to take in regards to my hospital test?" will do your physical (and mental) health more good than, "Will my hospital test come back positive or negative?"

For those times when you're not even sure what the issue is, let alone how to word the question: "What can I expect on a physical (emotional, mental, spiritual, or all of the above) level in my life in the next (few weeks, three days, five hours, etc.)," or, "What should I focus on this (week, month, quarter, etc.)?" will give you information you can do something with.

Think of formulating questions for the cards as skillful conversation. If you ask someone whether or not they liked a particular painting at the art museum, the dialogue might very well end there. But if you ask what they noticed about the painting, what effect the imagery had on them or how they see themselves in relationship to the artist's landscape, you'll not only get the answer you were originally seeking, but also the opportunity to explore and understand that person (and yourself) a whole lot better in the process.

As your Tarot adventures continue, and you come to know your surroundings and the language of the locals, you'll begin to "feel" your questions rather than think them. The issue at hand will simply rise to your inner eye, colored by imagination and curiosity, and the cards will weave their stories accordingly. You'll pull out the formal questions now and again, but as your connection deepens, your dialogue will become more and more instinctual, your experience with the cards more and more intimate. (Think of the wordless communication that happens between longtime lovers, versus the inquisitive exchange of first-time friends.)

This is a natural part of the mastering process and it will happen in its own season; there is no calendar when being the sorcerer's apprentice, and you'll be up to your eyeballs in magic either way, so sit back and enjoy the ride.

FIVE

# Open Your Mouth and Start Talking!

## Doing a Reading

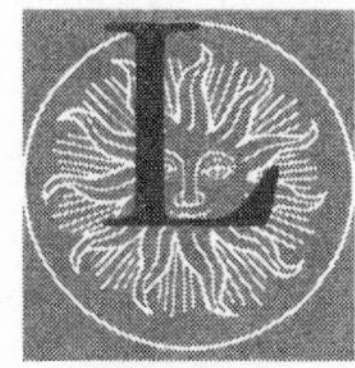

Lady Frieda Harris, the artist who painted the cards for Aleister Crowley's *Thoth* deck, described the Tarot as "God's picture book." Each card you turn is another page, and the message unfolds, image by image, according to the story's design. Reading that story is what this chapter is all about.

We've talked about the layers of information gleaned through the cards' imagery; we've shuffled and focused and worded our questions wisely. Now, we're going to lay the cards on the table, so to speak, and see what they have to say.

## spreads versus "Throwing" cards

A Tarot spread is an ordered layout of cards, with each card placed in a specific position, each position corresponding to a particular subject or point of focus. There are dozens of different spreads, forming complex patterns of pyramids, mandalas, crosses, wheels, or simply drawing the cards out in single rows. The individual cards are then interpreted within the context of their positions, and in accordance with the spread's defined meaning.

Two examples: In a Past-Present-Future spread, the first card is placed on the left, and is meant to symbolize influences or experiences of the past; the second card, placed in the middle, represents the present circumstance and its components; the third card, placed to the right, is the potential future outcome of the inquiry. Then you have the Mind-Body-Spirit spread, a similar three-card layout, with the mental influences or effects of a situation represented by the card on the left, the physical influences in the middle, and the emotional/spiritual influences on the right. These two spreads are among the simplest; the classic "Celtic Cross" spread uses ten to eleven cards in specific order, and I've seen others that call for upward of twenty.

Personally, I never use spreads. For me, their specific structure and linear scripting of the cards makes for too narrow a field of vision, and my intuition likes room to run. I prefer to just "throw" the cards—laying them out on the table according to what instinctively feels right at the time, and interpreting the images individually and collectively as they relate to one another and to the question at hand. Sometimes the cards just end up in a big patchwork pile; other times a distinct pattern appears, offering up its own layer of information.

In my classes I encourage students to pull no more than three to five cards for any given question; more than that can set the stage for confusion when you're first learning to work with the cards intuitively. I also advocate laying the cards out in a single row and reading them left to right, like a sentence. Once you've become a little more adept at swimming in the psychic sea, you can toss the cards all over the place if you like, as many as you like, and play with the placement as well as the imagery.

In chapter 12 we'll talk more about intuitive placement, and we'll also explore the three spreads mentioned previously—Past-Present-Future, Mind-Body-Spirit, and the Celtic Cross—just to experience the other side of the tracks. Remember, there is no wrong way to work with the Tarot. Spreads can be fun and "easy," in that they limit the psychic horizon to fit within their boundaries. Fewer options, shorter trip. Throwing the cards allows for a more free-form exchange between the images and your instincts, opening the way for a lot more psychic information, and making the journey a lot more interesting, in my opinion. Either way, it's an adventure. So, grab your deck, take a deep breath, and let's go for a little test drive. . . .

## Laying out the cards

Shuffle your cards, face down, concentrating a moment on your question; draw three, and lay them out *face up* in a row, left to right, beginning with the first card drawn. (Another rule I overthrow: Placing the cards face down on the table and turning them over one at a time to interpret. While there is a certain element of intrigue with this method, I prefer to see the imagery of the cards all at once, and all together, because I never know which symbol might spark me first and start the intuitive ball rolling.)

First off, simply notice the cards you pulled. Let your eye be drawn to whatever entreats it; view the cards through the lens of your question, allowing the imagery to synchronize and present itself to you. *Feel* it. (I know, I know . . . sounds all "New Age-y," doesn't it? Just give it a shot.) Now, if there is one place where I break my own rule regarding no rules, it's here: Open your mouth and start talking. I mean it. Even if you're alone in your room pulling cards in the closet, do your reading out loud. It's the single most effective way I have found to bypass the intellect and engage the intuitive soul.

If you sit and look at the cards in silence for too long, you'll start *thinking* about them. (Sort of like standing in front of an empty canvas with a creative idea bouncing around in your head—if you don't pick up a paintbrush, eventually the idea will atrophy, and you'll end up standing there forever.) This is an open invitation to The Committee, and believe me, they are always the first to arrive at the party, and absolutely the last to leave. So even if you have no earthly idea what to say, then say that! Start with anything; speak about the color of the sky behind the Two of Swords, or the way the Prince of Cup's cloak is spread behind him like wings . . . just begin.

Start with the first card you pulled; free-associate with colors, clouds, body language, terrain. Does the scene portrayed remind you of anything from your own experience? Perhaps the King of Pentacles bears a resemblance to your new boss, or the landscape in the Four of Wands takes you back to childhood summers at your grandparents' farm. Let the characters in the cards become the players of your inquiry, and ask *them* what they have to say. *You* get to play detective—hunting for symbolic clues in the scenery, analyzing the attitude and expressions of the card's inhabitants, and creating a dialogue as you piece the puzzle together.

Remember, the cards are telling you a story. As narrator, it's your job to move with it; from the first to the second card, and to the third, connecting the images and giving them a voice. I promise you, opening your mouth will open a doorway to great and mysterious things that might otherwise remain locked, perhaps always, in the castle tower of your doubting mind.

This process is very like automatic writing—channeling Divine guidance through writing without conscious intent, using your non-dominant hand. The first time I tried automatic writing, I thought, *Yeah, right.* I didn't have the vaguest idea how, or even if, it was going to work. But I picked up my pen anyway, started my first sentence with "I have no idea what I'm doing with this I just wanted to see what would happen . . ." and *Boom!* The pen was off and scampering across the paper and I was racing to catch up, completely astonished at what was coming through. The *action* of expressing—through language, through voice or paintbrush or pen—is like opening the gate on a thoroughbred, poised to run, that's been trained and waiting all his life for that bell to finally go off.

The most important thing, and by far the most difficult, is to trust the information you receive. And unfortunately, there's no magic bullet for that one. Trust is the spiritual Nike commercial—Just Do It. And then keep doing it, over and over, until you fortify your intuitive muscle and it can begin to stand on its own. Working with the Tarot is the perfect strength-training drill.

## A Sample Reading

Following is an example of just how intuitive information can filter through the images in a Tarot card. This is a one-card reading.

You're thinking about leaving your current corporate job for something more creative, but you fear taking the professional risk. You shuffle the deck and draw a single card: the Queen of Wands dances across the table. You're immediately charmed by the bright fire colors of this card's imagery; the feeling evoked is one of playfulness and passion, exactly what you're looking for in a new career. The Queen's blond mane is unbound and wind-blown, her clothing loose and flowing around her. *That* feels like freedom, and you find your heart begins to beat a little faster. Next, describing the sunflowers at the Queen's feet, springing from desert sand, you can see how your creativity has been withering in a work environment every bit as barren as the pictured landscape.

And then you recall a recent conversation in which a good friend advised you to "take matters into your own hands" and make a change. You study the wand in the Queen's hand, bright and electric, feeling her posture and expression of regal confidence. Hmmm. Coincidence? Hardly. More like a spiritual confirmation call. But the risks involved, you argue—what of that? *That's* when you notice that the Queen's gown is embroidered with the head of a roaring lion, and a scene from the Wizard of Oz pops unbidden into your mind . . . the Cowardly Lion, singing about courage.

With an open mind and an inquisitive eye, amazing amounts of serendipitous wisdom can be gleaned from a single card. Look what can be had when you weave together the imagery of three:

## A Second Sample Reading

You've recently fallen in love with the perfect little Victorian house; you've made an offer, and now you're waiting to find out if it will be accepted and if the financing will go through. What can you expect in the next few weeks regarding this process?

The first card up is Justice—a proud and regal woman seated between two pillars, wearing a cloak of red and purple; she holds a set of scales in one hand, a sword in the other. Next is Temperance—a broad-winged angel, standing with one foot in water, the other on land, juggling three polished globes in perfect rhythm. The third card is the Six of Swords—a boat carved in the shape of a great swan, moving across a body of water to a nearing shoreline; there are six swords flanking the neck of the swan, three to each side, and between them sits the figure of a young man.

You lay the cards out, noticing their coloration and mood, individually and as a collage. Lots of blues and greens; there is a clear sense of strength and calm with this layout, and as you bring that feeling into your body, it actually makes your spine straighten, your breathing grow deeper. Nothing to recoil at here!

The Justice card seems almost too obvious. The card's title, the scales and the sword, and the judiciary bearing of the robed woman, all easily combine to conjure legal documents and real estate contracts. There is an air of steady resolve about the imagery; the predominant crimson of the robe, quite vivid in comparison to the paler colors of the other two cards, feels to you like a surge of confidence and power. The fact that the scales are perfectly balanced also seems a positive sign, and the sword is upright, which makes you think of a "thumbs up," a signal that plans will indeed move ahead. Your eyes are drawn to the pillars; what are they saying to you? Perhaps they merely symbolize support for the process, you say, especially since they appear slightly behind the woman, almost protectively guarding her. . . . Then suddenly you are reminded of the columns that flank the gingerbread doorway of your dream house. Ah, a little scattering of faerie dust appears. . . .

Temperance seems a bit tougher to interpret. So you begin with describing the blue sky and the white mist of clouds on the horizon; then you move on to the angel and the juggled globes; suddenly you see *yourself* juggling all the details that must be attended to in a real estate transaction—dealing with the bank and the mortgage broker, coordinating closing dates with moving plans, packing, paperwork, etc. The word *overwhelm* rises to mind (and the sensation threatens to follow), but then you notice the expression of calm on the angel's face, the fact that it's an *angel* (a little cosmic intervention is always a good sign!), and that he appears to be relaxed, with the juggling thing well under control. A quick flash of memory—a tiny gold angel with crystalline wings—the lapel pin your real estate agent was wearing the day she showed you the house. (More faerie dust!) This card seems to say, *Stay calm.* Manage the details that come up with a relaxed and steady rhythm, and trust that you're in good hands, literally.

The very first thing you notice in the Six of Swords is movement, as opposed to the steadfast positions of Justice and the angel of Temperance. The water beneath the boat is rippled and rough; beyond the boat, the way is smooth as the glass globes in the angel's hands. How does the image of the boat and the water relate to your question? You see it as moving through the challenges of the buying process, staying afloat, as it were; you picture the actual move into the new house, and the term "smooth sailing" comes to mind. You study the figure of the young man, but nothing tugs at you; instead, you're drawn to the swords that surround him. . . . Look closer. The hilts, gothic and ornate, appear very similar to the wrought iron finials on the gate leading to your new front door. And, as you now recall (with a big, toothy grin), there happen to be exactly six finials on that magical gate, thank you very much. Faerie dust *everywhere!*

## And Now for something with a Bit More Bite . . .

Your divorce was final a year ago; you've been back in the dating game for some time, to no avail, and your patience is wearing thin. What can you expect in the realm of romance in the next few months?

The Devil shows up first. It literally flies out of the deck as you're shuffling, spinning to a stop on the table in front of you, upright and ready to talk—a man and a woman standing naked in a darkened tunnel, holding to opposite ends of an ornate chest bound with iron chains and filled with riches, struggling with the overflowing treasure and against one another. The second card is the Four of Wands, which depicts the seemingly identical couple (she with flowing red hair, he with blonde, in both cases), this time cheerfully clothed, dancing with one another in graceful rhythm beneath a garland-draped canopy. The third card you draw is Death—a figure clad in a scarlet robe, standing at the juncture of converging paths that wind through a green wood, holding a banner depicting a single white rose on a black background.

The collective imagery of this layout isn't exactly cringe-worthy, but you do find yourself tensing somewhat, having hoped for a bit more sunshine and flowers, considering the subject. The tone of this layout feels serious, a little like sitting in the principal's office, waiting for a lecture you know you probably deserve. Are you ready to receive the information that's presenting itself? The cards are already out.... Might as well take a look.

What immediately leaps to your eye in this layout is the connection between the Devil and the Four of Wands—there is no escaping the fact that it is the same couple portrayed on both cards, and the contrast in energy and environment between the two scenarios makes for an explicit commentary on the duality of relationship and the power of choice. The scene depicted in the Four of Wands is what you're hoping for in a future relationship; the scene in the Devil is uncomfortably true to how your marriage looked before it ended. You see yourself and your ex in the months that led up to the divorce—trapped by anger, clutching at possessions, refusing to see each other's pain and confusion. As you study the cards, the emotions of that time rise in you, still as strong and as tangled as the chains that bind the couple in the Devil's darkened corridor; the Four of Wands looks suddenly like an illusion, a masquerade of happiness that hides a deeper truth.

The Death card, rather than appearing ominous next to the Four, seems sad, almost impatient. "Time to move on," the cloaked figure might be saying. In this card, too, there is obvious choice; one path leads to the left, back toward the struggle and pretense of the Devil and the Four of Wands, the second path moves forward, perhaps toward a fresh horizon. Have you been holding on to your anger, to the drama of your breakup, even as you've been attempting to create something new?

You notice how green the forest is in the Death card, the yellow butterfly dancing at the figure's feet; you are reminded of the rhythms of nature, that spring always follows winter's sleep, that the caterpillar emerges from its own sort of death, irrevocably, blessedly changed. Then something about the symbol on the banner draws your eye—you remember an ad you saw in the Yellow Pages, with a logo of a single rose, for a counselor who specializes in grief and life transformation. What's it going to take for you to emerge from the cocoon of your current dating experience? Choosing to leave the past and your hurt behind and trusting that to everything there is indeed a season.

## getting clearer

Okay, so what happens if the information *doesn't* come through so easily? You lay out your cards, talk about the imagery, and find that you're stuck, drawing an absolute blank. Pull one more card and ask for clarity, either for the entire reading or for a particular card in the layout that's giving you trouble.

Let's take the Temperance card in the second sample reading for example. Say you just can't get past that blue sky and white misty horizon, so you draw another card, seeking insight into the juggling angel, and up pops the Three of Pentacles.

This card shows a man, smiling, working away with chisel and hammer, carving a great stone feather in a monolithic wing; three golden pentacles adorn the marble plumes. A master artist, you imagine, perhaps creating his greatest work. So how does this help demystify Temperance? Notice the wing motif repeating; this pulls you back to the notion of angelic intervention. The three pentacles correspond with the angel's juggling globes; the idea of juggling proved to be a key piece of emotional information in the reading, and this extra symbolism might just shake that analogy loose. Also, the posture and expression of the man, in control, not in the least bit hurried, paying obvious attention to detail with skill and patience—here we have our same experience of the Temperance card: staying calm, managing tasks one at a time, and being in the hands of a master.

If you've pulled one or two cards for clarity, and still the reading seems clouded, you might try rephrasing the question, or even waiting a bit and asking again at a later time. Psychic energy, and your ability to access it, can wax and wane just as any cycle in Nature. Sometimes you're just "on," and other times it can be harder to tap in; as you become more adept, your connection will become more consistent, regardless of circumstance. Still, certain planetary influences, environmental dynamics, even physical and emotional energy levels, can all have an effect on intuitive channels.

I find, almost without exception, that doing readings for clients actually elevates my mood; I get to step outside the confines of my own world (thus putting whatever's troubling me into perspective) and impart channeled wisdom that I can put to good use myself. Helping others find hope and inspiration to better their lives is powerful medicine for my own. But doing a reading for myself when I'm feeling out of sorts is usually a dead-end, at best; at worst, it adds frustration to an already frazzled humor. At those times I'll walk around the house with a deck in my hand, but not to draw cards or ask questions—simply to be comforted by their familiar energy.

It's especially difficult, if not downright impossible, to read the cards objectively when you have a strong personal attachment to the question. Life-changing decisions and issues of extreme emotional import, whether they concern yourself or someone you care for, are better left off-limits; when you find yourself too close for comfort, turn the reading over to someone you trust, and leave the lesser details of the issue to your own decks. My best friend Kim and I trade readings whenever we feel the need to get a second psychic "opinion," but both she and I regularly consult another mutual friend and trusted reader for the really big stuff. You'll have to be the judge of whether or not your mood impacts your ability to read—the more you work with the cards, the more you'll get to know your own rhythms, and know when it's appropriate to put the deck down and take a break or leave the reading in someone else's hands entirely.

Keeping a journal of your readings is a great way to chronicle those rhythms. It's also a powerful tool for recording and strengthening your intuitive voice. Log the question, as it was asked, the cards you pulled, and your (spoken aloud!) interpretation. Later, if you find you were off in your answer, you can re-evaluate the reading in light of how the experience actually unfolded. You'll be amazed to find how accurate the cards were after all—and have yet another opportunity to see the myriad ways the imagery of a single card might be construed.

In a Tarot journal you can track your favorite and least favorite cards, create an expanding "database" of personal interpretations and triggers, and keep account of outcome as well as timelines. There were several readings I did when first starting out that I would have sworn were going to unfold precisely as I'd seen them, yet didn't; it wasn't until much later that I went back, looked over the journal entry, and realized they had indeed come to pass in that exact manner, only with a different time frame than I had divined. (Timelines are coming up in chapter 12.) You'll also want a journal to record the goose bump-provoking, eerily obvious spiritual messages and life-altering experiences that I guarantee working with the Tarot will produce.

This brings me to one final point regarding readings: the two aspects of the psyche that will always be present with you when you throw the cards. The first is Doubt, who will stand at your shoulder, close enough to tickle your ear with his breath, and insist that you can't possibly know what you're saying, that the still, quiet whisper of intuition that has just begun to rise in you is only your "imagination," that you are wrong, wrong, *Wrong*. (I'm pretty sure that, unlike The Committee, Doubt works solo . . . but I guarantee they all belong to the same Union.) He still circles the room sometimes when I'm doing readings, even after all these years, pacing back and forth in front of windows; he can even fool me into closing my mouth on occasion. Doubt isn't intentionally cruel; he's merely trying to keep you on your toes and protect you from—*gasp!*—Enlightenment, and therefore, Change. Thank him for his input and send him out for pizza.

And then there is Wonder, who always waits by the door, eyes wide and luminous; until you invite her in, she won't participate, only observe. You'll feel her, even at that distance, slightly breathless, poised on tiptoe, ready without question to witness magic. Ask her to pull up a chair and let her draw a card or two; pretty soon, she'll be dancing in your living room and hanging out in your life as if she's lived there, always. It will be up to you to welcome her home.

SIX

# The Language of Secrets and Symbols

## Discovering the Essential Energies of the Cards

A sovereign queen, seated on a throne carved of abalone and pearl, her sea-foam robes billowing over golden sand. A warrior, returning to his homeland on the back of a storm-colored stallion, a wreath of laurel on his head and a flag of victory streaming from his hand. Two beggars, clothed in rags, huddled in a snow-covered courtyard; just beyond them, the gothic stained glass of a cathedral window, glowing with hope and lamplight. A castle on a distant hill; birds in a V against a pale winter sky; an arbor in a garden hung heavy with fruit and roses.

No words, only images—emotional, evocative, inviting memories, passions, curiosity. The system of language found in the Tarot is wholly symbolic, creating a pictorial treatise of archetype and universal experience. The symbology of the Tarot is part of its enduring history; even the most avant-garde of decks contains at least some of the original representations. This allegorical language portrays what has been called "the collective myths of mankind"—chronicling the evolution and psychology of the spiritual human from innocence to enlightenment.

Remember the analogy of the archaeologist's dig in chapter 3? In this chapter, we're going to explore one of those layers of mystical information—the messages inherent in the timeless symbolism of the Tarot.

I'm going to offer up these messages in simple listings of three words or phrases for each card. *These are not definitions!* They're triggers, meant to jumpstart emotional response. Use them merely as suggestion, possibility, discourse; bounce them off of an intuitive block and see if they'll nudge open the door. Read the cards instinctively first, then add the following information as a garnish—and only if it will complement your original recipe. In other words, if to you a bird does not symbolize an idea, but rather, feels more like a visitation from an otherworldly guide, then that is the most important interpretation, and the "idea" idea should take second fiddle.

## The Major Arcana

The cards of the Major Arcana are considered by some to be the most important cards in the deck; there are even a few decks on the market today that contain *only* the Major Arcana—the cards numbered zero through twenty-one—which depict spiritual archetypes and higher truths.

I usually experience the appearance of Major Arcana cards in a layout as a sort of mystical postscript, telling me that something greater is afoot regarding the subject at hand. After I've interpreted a layout intuitively, I'll take a second to notice the number of Major Arcana cards, and perhaps their placement in the layout if I'm drawn to that; the more Major Arcana cards in a particular grouping, the more import I believe the experience depicted contains, and the greater the spiritual lesson or opportunity to be had.

For instance, if someone comes up in a reading as the Magician or the Emperor, as opposed to the King of Swords or a soldier in the Seven of Wands, it may be that the question is more a soul issue than a human one, or perhaps there's a karmic influence in need of clarification. As always, it depends entirely upon the reading; sometimes the Major Arcana cards show up as MAJOR ARCANA CARDS, and sometimes they just weave themselves simply and quietly into the mix.

Following are some of the different impressions one might gather from the twenty-two trump cards of the Major Arcana:

0 *The Fool:* Innocence. Faith. Beginnings.

1 *The Magician:* Creativity. Guile. Personal power.

2 *The High Priestess:* Intuition. Calm. Spiritual assistance.

3 *The Empress:* Nurturing. Receptivity. Divine Mother.

4 *The Emperor:* Leadership. Discipline. Divine Father.

5 *The Hierophant:* Knowledge. Tradition. Structure.

6 *The Lovers:* Union. Choice. Relationship.

7 *The Chariot:* Movement. Triumph. Travel.

8 *Strength:* Willpower. Recovery. Success.

9 *The Hermit:* Wisdom. Introspection. Spiritual guidance.

10 *The Wheel of Fortune:* Destiny. Chance. Karma.

11 *Justice:* Balance. Fairness. Legal systems.

12 *The Hanged Man:* Surrender. Release. Timing.

13 *Death:* Rebirth. Renewal. Cycles.

14 *Temperance:* Patience. Cooperation. Inaction.

15 *The Devil:* Fear. Attachment. Desire.

16 *The Tower:* Change. Opportunity. Awareness.

17 *The Star:* Peace. Compassion. Miracles.

18 *The Moon:* Mystery. Imagination. The Goddess.

19 *The Sun:* Vitality. Creativity. The God.

20 *Judgment:* Revelation. Freedom. Enlightenment.

21 *The World:* Completion. Attainment. Mastery.

## The Minor Arcana

The remaining fifty-six cards in the Tarot deck are the pip cards of the Minor Arcana. While the Major Arcana cards represent the properties of

Spirit and the mystical journey of the soul, the Minor Arcana cards are considered to be snapshots of the human experience—emotions, actions, thoughts, expressions, events—representing the more mundane demonstrations of everyday life. Each of the four suits of the Minor Arcana contain the Ace through Ten cards, as well as the four Court cards—the Page or Princess, the Knight or Prince, the Queen, and the King. The Ace through Ten of each suit have their individual numeric energies, the Court cards have "personality" types, and the four suits are similar to the correspondences used in Wiccan spell work and ritual.[1]

## THE FOUR SUITS

The four suits of the Minor Arcana are Wands, Cups, Pentacles, and Swords. Note that different decks may have other names for the suits, such as Rods or Staves instead of Wands; Hearts rather than Cups; Disks or Coins instead of Pentacles; Crystals or Spears rather than Swords. Following are a few of the elemental and energetic correspondences associated with each of the different suits.

*Wands:* Fire. Spiritual. Passion. Sexuality. Creativity. Action. Enterprise. Leadership. Identity.

*Cups:* Water. Emotional. Feelings. Moods. Romance. Creativity. Dreams. Fantasy.

*Pentacles:* Earth. Physical. Tangible. Money. Health. Business. Structure. Reality.

---

[1]See Michele Morgan, *Simple Wicca,* Conari Press, 2000.

*Swords:* Air. Mental. Thoughts. Ideas. Communication. Truth. Justice. Objectivity.

Another way of interpreting the energy of the suits is through the correspondences of direction and season. Tradition holds to the suit of Wands ruling Summer and the South; Cups, Autumn and the West; Pentacles, Winter and the North; and Swords, Spring and the East. Suffice it to say, if this works for you, use it. If not, find your own compass.

Once I took a class on ritual study in which we learned the "rules" of setting up an altar using the four directions as the energetic foundation. Right out of the gate I found myself dyslexic regarding East and West and their symbolic intent; my instincts were in an uproar of rebellion until the instructor finally sighed and told me to "do it my way," which was completely backward, but resulted in some astonishingly powerful magic! This of course led to several others in the class breaking out of the conventional mold, much to the teacher's chagrin, and forging unique connections to their spiritual selves that might otherwise have been greatly stifled. I'm such a troublemaker!

In chapter 12, we'll be playing with timelines and thus intuiting seasons; for now, let yourself connect to the imagery of the suits as it suits *you.*

### ACE THROUGH TEN

Following are a few of the numeric qualities associated with the Minor Arcana cards; you might consult a numerology book for a more in-depth exploration.

*Ace:* Beginning. Originality. Renewal.

*Two:* Balance. Cooperation. Patience.

*Three:* Growth. Self-expression. Expansion.

*Four:* Structure. Security. Stability.

*Five:* Change. Action. Challenge.

*Six:* Harmony. Responsibility. Objectivity.

*Seven:* Intuition. Knowledge. Introspection.

*Eight:* Activity. Achievement. Advancement.

*Nine:* Wisdom. Spirituality. Enlightenment.

*Ten:* Completion. Tradition. Mastery.

### THE COURT CARDS

The Court cards can be seen as a representation of personality type or elements of self-mastery. For example, the Page or Princess is considered to be the student of his or her particular suit, the Knight or Prince is the explorer or adventurer, the Queen is the nurturer, and the King is the manifester. As we discussed in chapter 3, tradition holds to the Court cards representing a particular person, with particular personality traits, exclusively; for me, this is a limiting and often confusing parameter. I'd rather see you explore the images of the Court cards intuitively first, and see what stories they might wish to tell before holding them to a designated role in your reading. Following are a few qualities you might consider when exploring these cards.

*Page or Princess:* Messages. Youth. Naïveté.

*Knight or Prince:* Protection. Strength. Determination.

*Queen:* Maturity. Competence. Devotion.

*King:* Mastery. Wisdom. Control.

### INDIVIDUAL SYMBOLS

Following are just a few examples of specific symbols that can be found in most Tarot decks. Another source for symbolic definitions are books on dream interpretation, such as *The Hidden Power of Dreams* by Denise Linn.

*Angels:* Higher self. Spiritual protection. Wisdom.

*Animals* (general): Lower self. Physical needs. Instinct. (Individual animals have different symbolic "traits," such as Horses representing power, or Rabbits representing abundance; this can also vary according to culture and mythology. Sources such as *The Medicine Cards* by Jamie Sams, *The Druid Animal Oracle* by Philip and Stephanie Carr-Gomm, or *Animal Wise Tarot* by Ted Andrews are great resources for animal symbology.)

*Birds* (general): Ideas. Messages. Spirit. (Again, different birds, different energies. Hawk is a messenger, Raven is magic, Owl is intuition. See *Animals* for sources.)

*Buildings:* Security. Structure. Tradition.

*Butterfly:* Transformation. Freedom. Fragility.

*Clouds:* Emotions. Ideas. Dreams.

*Crown:* Divinity. Spiritual illumination. Victory.

*Fish:* The unconscious. Dreams. Creation.

*Flowers* (general): Abundance. Fertility. Beauty. (Check sources such as Scott Cunningham's *Encyclopedia of Magical Herbs: A Victorian Grimoire* by Patricia Telesco, or *The Wicca Garden* by Gerina Dunwich for the symbolism of specific flowers.)

*Hills:* Minor challenges. Journeys. Awareness.

*Ivy:* Luck. Protection. Fidelity. (See Flowers regarding sources for individual plants.)

*Moon:* The Goddess. Intuition. Imagination.

*Mountains:* Major challenges. Wisdom. Strength.

*Rivers:* Emotional flux. Progress. Spiritual quest.

*Road:* Spiritual journey. Choice. Consciousness.

*Rocks:* Obstacles. Stability. Possessions.

*Stars:* Angelic presence. Illumination. Life force.

*Sun:* The God. Courage. Creative power.

*Wheat:* Abundance. Sustenance. Wealth.

*Wheel:* Divine power. Completion. The cosmos.

*Wreath:* Victory. Wealth. The Goddess.

## COLOR ASSOCIATIONS

Color carries symbolic impact. Here are just a few examples; check out books on color or candle magic and ritual for more.

*White:* Purity. Brilliance. Renewal.

*Red:* Strength. Life force. Power.

*Orange:* Vitality. Courage. Passion.

*Yellow:* Creativity. Confidence. Glory.

*Green:* Health. Fertility. Money.

*Blue:* Spiritual inspiration. Wisdom. Peace.

*Indigo:* Self-mastery. Prophecy. Protection.

*Violet:* Spiritual mastery. Protection. Healing.

*Brown:* Earth. Death. Physical realm.

*Black:* Mystery. Protection. The unknown.

*Remember:* Use the mini-symbolic "expressions" found in this chapter to expand your vision of the cards, not define it. Another way to make good use of your Tarot journal—create your own glossary of symbols and record all the various connections and impressions they afford you.

# PART II

# Heart and Soul

# introduction

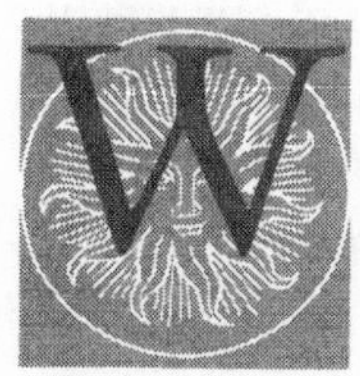

elcome to the most controversial portion of this book; the part most anticipated by the reader and most eschewed by me . . . the section no Tarot book would be complete without. In fact, it's the section most Tarot books *revolve* around—I'll even wager a few of you went straight to this part of the book *first*. Those of you, guilty-as-charged, know who you are. (Probably Sagittarians!) For the rest of you curious but patient seekers, know that you stand at the threshold of an ancient and mystical tradition—the unveiling of (drum roll, please!) the definitions of the Tarot cards.

Alright, so I'm being dramatic. I just want to reiterate (belabor, harp on, *drive into your heads*) that the definitions are only one piece of the proverbial Tarot pie. To that end, what follows in this chapter are less definitions and more *interpretations*, written from a storyteller's perspective. The strength of the Tarot lies in its ability to capture the imagination and to entreat the seeker to explore strange and fairytale horizons; having those horizons too clearly defined bleeds the magic and the life from the journey. Simple, poetic, visual, as impassioned as the images themselves, the descriptions of the cards should coax the storyline of a reading along, not determine its every intrigue.

Accordingly, I was inspired. I loved writing about the cards, imagining their characters' personalities and passions, depicting them as principals in a fable or in a minstrel's song. And, so, the accompanying illustrations serve to feed that fairytale concept as well, penned by the lyrical hand of Rebecca Richards, an extraordinary artist who also happens to be my dear friend. That Beck and I could collaborate on this labor of love was a gift in and of itself; exploring the landscape of our creative connection, above and beyond our friendship, made for blissful hours of brainstorming, laughter, and an uncanny symmetry of vision.

Rebecca's ability to translate that vision into the exquisite pen-and-ink drawings found here is also a gift—you won't find these images anywhere else. They don't belong to any existing Tarot deck, nor are they intended to become one. Instead, these illustrations are an imprint of the essential energy of each Tarot card, meant to incite, inspire, evoke, and conjure, inviting emotional response so that intuition is guaranteed to come out and play. Rebecca's drawings are like jewels, tiny presents wrapped in gilded paper and dragonflies' wings, opening themselves anew every time you open this book.

Beginning with the Major Arcana, and moving through the suits of Wands, Cups, Pentacles, and Swords, the illustrations capture the heart of the Tarot; the narratives give voice to its soul. These interpretive discourses are not absolutes—they are energetic in nature, descriptive of element and possibility, meant to stimulate and expand upon your own intuitive perception of the cards. They may ultimately have nothing at all to add to what the cards are saying to you in a reading—like any written definition, these are simply *my* interpretations, sprung from the Tarot's history and from my experience with, understanding of, and emotional connection to the cards. So, like everything else in this or any Tarot book, please feel free to take what works for you and leave the rest.

Like the symbolic correspondences in chapter 6, use these images and descriptions to illuminate ever-deeper layers of emotion and insight within the cards, guided first by your imagination and psychic senses. Let your mind wander and your heart explore, but remember: *There will be no definition in any book stronger than your own instinctual understanding of the cards.*

All that said, turn the page and draw the curtain aside....

# SEVEN

# The Major Arcana

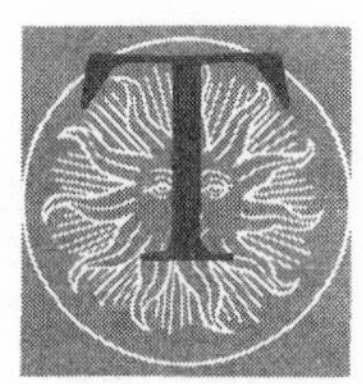

The Major Arcana cards contain some of the most mystical images in the Tarot deck. These are the characters inherent in the human psyche, the archetypes that belong to the collective unconscious—priest, goddess, judge, teacher, mother, father, angel, demon. The twenty-two trump cards of the Major Arcana present a vivid portrait of the process of alchemy—the transformation of something common (human) into something extraordinary (Spirit).

Illustrated through the cyclical nature of all things—life and death, sleep and resurrection, strength and struggle, light and dark—each card of the Major Arcana represents a particular stage of spiritual development, from the innocence and candor of the Fool, to the mastery and attainment of the World. Of course, as in the eternal spiral of life, an ending is always followed by a new beginning. Once mastery is reached, the student emerges yet again, fresh to the next experience but made wiser from the last, and the soul continues to evolve, without cease, toward enlightenment.

## 0 The Fool

The Fool represents innocence. Here is the start of the journey, the creative odyssey where the only goal is enlightenment and the only rule is faith. This is where magic begins, where the landscape takes on the colors of a child's paint box, the Earth forever poised just this side of spring, where instinct and simplicity escape from ego, and the intellect becomes drunk on the scent of possibility. This is Nature's first green; skipping through the garden gate with the wisdom and whimsy of youth. With the Fool you find fresh starts, renewed energy, and second chances. Wherever you are, there is your true beginning.

# 1 The Magician

The Magician symbolizes creation. A fire is kindled, then fueled, then tempered by a single hand. What appeared to you before as merely thought or idle fancy now dances and breathes, alive at your feet. Here you learn to conduct the elements of intellect, Spirit, Earth, and emotion—tools to bring life and energy to whatever you desire. With the Magician come passion and focus, mastery over self and circumstance, and the discovery of once untapped resources and abilities with which to transform the mundane into the extraordinary. This is power and its right use; this is the true nature of Magic.

## 2 The High Priestess

The High Priestess embodies the intuitive. Here is the still, blue space deep within you, where the clamor of logic and ego give way beneath the rhythms of wind and water and the slow, quiet turning of the stars. Intuition speaks in a whisper, preferring color and texture to language and sound, moonlight to street lamps, empathy and trust to control. With this card you are invited to partake of blood and spirit, to participate in your own mythology, to quiet yourself and re-establish your kinship with the Divine. Trust what you feel, and you will find that the questions answer themselves.

## 3 The Empress

The Empress is the nurturer. With this card you not only experience the process of conception, gestation, and birth but also provide the guidance and care needed to assure sustained growth. Here is the nursemaid, smoothing a pale brow, administering comfort and herbs to bring a fever into balance; the gardener, carefully coaxing a shy seedling bed into riotous flower; the artist, curving gentle hands through clay and water, to impart earthly form with imagination. Patience and love, creativity and wisdom, the capacity to give and receive with a balanced heart—these are all qualities of the Empress, the quintessential Earth Mother.

## 4 The Emperor

The Emperor defines leadership. Fearless and visionary, his path is a noble one, seeking enlightenment and the good of all above his own. He is the champion who lifts his sword not for the taste of blood or victory but to redress the suffering of a comrade. This is the warrior who maps the battlefield, plans the strategies, organizes the ranks, then prays with and comforts the soldiers before fronting the charge. With this card you experience force tempered with compassion, power born of integrity, and strength and authority without conceit. This is the first nature of power and the totem of true mastery.

## 5 The Hierophant

The Hierophant symbolizes knowledge and guidance, both earthly and Divine. This is the energy of spiritual connection and life mentors, the chance meeting on the street corner with a wise and prophetic stranger; the aging master, inspiring the youthful apprentice on the journey toward his own mastery. Here you find history, warming the stone path in a monastery garden, gilding the dusty bookshelves of an ivy-covered hall, sifting through the colored panes of an ancient cathedral window. With this card you experience the power of ritual, the comfort of tradition and sacred law, and the significance of being both student and sage.

## 6 The Lovers

The Lovers is a card of balance and union, as reflected in the realm of personal relationship. Here we find the language of fairy tales, the "happily ever after" where the knight rescues the maiden fair. This is the alchemy of partnership or sacred marriage—the blending of two energies into a third, magical force. Choice is often indicated by this card as well: a decision between one or more possible people or experiences; or between the fantasy of the knight and maiden and the reality of the boy or girl next door. Whether in love, business, or the kingdom of self, your relationships mirror your inner balance.

## 7 The Chariot

The Chariot represents the energy of movement and change. There is a feeling of great power and strength with this card as well as the recognition of having overcome hardship to attain it. Here is mastery over external forces. With the Chariot, opposition is met with courage, and triumph prevails by the force of your own determination and will. Assurance, bravado, self-control, and discipline are all weapons you have brandished to this end. This card symbolizes a moment to reflect before continuing on your path, confident in the direction and flying the colors of your experience proudly.

## 8 strength

Strength is a card of power and self-discipline. This is the story of the beautiful maiden who tames the wild beast, not with force or cruelty but with love. By recognizing the good inherent in all things, she calms the raging animal with gentle acceptance and turns it from an adversary into an ally. Just as this myth symbolizes mastery over fear, so this card symbolizes understanding and conquering your own inner "beasts," which include negative, self-defeating, or addictive thoughts or behaviors. Spiritual insight and courage are your weapons; faith and love your shield. The outcome? Integrity of body, mind, and soul.

## 9 The Hermit

The Hermit is a symbol of introspection and the wisdom that is gleaned in thoughtful silence. This card invites you to withdraw from the clutter and commotion of the everyday world and find peace in solitude. Reflection, re-evaluation, and spiritual study are the tools; connecting to that which is sacred and meaningful becomes the inspiration. The Hermit is the wise one, the tribal elder, the ancient sage who lives alone on the rocky cliff side, to whom hundreds make the long pilgrimage on foot to seek true counsel. Retreat for a time into his realm; learn his ways of careful deliberation, self-knowledge, and prudence in thought and deed, and then carry his teachings like a lantern to light your world when you return.

## 10 The Wheel of Fortune

The Wheel of Fortune is a universal symbol of destiny or karma. The message of this card is to think before you act, as everything you do "comes back to you threefold." Luck and chance are also represented by the Wheel, as are the cycles of life and death, fortune and poverty. Take responsibility for your fate and be open to any new or unexpected opportunities. This card often portends a major turning point, an advantageous sequence of events, or a time for progress and advancement in any arena. Don't be afraid to take risks; the Wheel is turning in your favor.

## 11 Justice

Justice symbolizes the importance of balance, of seeing all sides of any situation before making a decision. This card represents Divine judgment as an angel of mercy, armed with sword and scale, who weighs the opposing elements and dispenses fair and fitting sentence. Legal matters, arbitration, and contracts of all kinds are implicated here. This card also speaks of being held accountable for your past and reaping what you have sown. So arm yourself with virtue and integrity, and stand righteous in the face of tyranny, to defend and honor your truth. Have faith that Justice will prevail.

## 12 The Hanged Man

The Hanged Man is a symbol of release. Here is an opportunity to change your perspective, to view the world through different eyes. This card indicates a time of waiting, of sacrificing yourself to a higher purpose, just as a caterpillar waits in its cocoon, surrendering to the natural process of transformation and change. Release comes only when the change is complete, when the watercolor wings split their silken cage and the caterpillar engages the world from its brand new disposition. Acceptance, enlightenment, inspiration, wisdom; surrender to the process and learn to fly.

## 13 Death

Death symbolizes the experience of rebirth and renewal and the cycles inherent in all of life. The planets turn in a slow orbit of seasons—the barren sleep of winter always leading the Earth into the warmth and resurgence of spring; the moon lives and dies, and lives again, holding oceans and lovers captive in her spell. With this card comes an awareness of your own cycles of life and death; letting go of outmoded patterns of behavior and thought, the ending of relationships or experiences, in order to create the space and energy essential for new expression.

## 14 Temperance

Temperance symbolizes the energies of patience and discipline. The success of any venture depends upon the proper combination of components, married with tenacity and timing. This card speaks of such a blend, with the aid of cooperation, balance, modification, and natural law. The integration of opposing elements to create harmony; the synthesis of physical and spiritual principles; adjusting to circumstance to allow an unrestrained flow of energy. Temperance is the alchemy of creativity and invention and contains the formula for true success.

## 15 The Devil

The Devil symbolizes the self-imprisonment created by negative thought patterns or internal beliefs. This card presents a mask of fear and an opportunity to face that fear and come to terms with it so that it no longer dominates you. The Devil comes in other guises as well: greed, jealousy, obsession, materialism, vanity—all are veils that prevent your true self from experiencing the world. The message of this card is to release yourself from emotional bondage, to change your focus from the external, material realm to that of the spiritual, and to confront the energies that hold you captive to your own imposed limitations. Remove the mask and set yourself free.

## 16 The Tower

The Tower is a card of radical change. Lightning strikes; a fortress crumbles. All that has ceased to serve you, either conscious or unconscious, is being swept away, the canvas wiped clean for the artist's greater vision. Here is opportunity and growth, unexpected awareness, a sudden chance to dramatically alter the landscape of your future. It is a brief moment, like a storm in mid-summer—the vital life force of creativity and courage gone nova. *Carpe Diem!*

## 17 The Star

The Star illustrates spiritual and creative expression. With this card comes enlightenment and peace, illumination of your soul's purpose, and recognition of your talents and artistic potential. This is the mythology of guardian angels, fairy godmothers, and granted wishes. With the Star you experience both sides of the story, as benefactor and recipient. This card finds you influencing others to positive ends, bringing to light some altruistic or humanitarian ideal, or finding the proper channels through which to begin pursuing your life's work. The Star heralds a time where potential becomes actuality, and dreams become real.

## 18 The Moon

The Moon is a harbinger of mystery and change. This card rules the subconscious, proffering messages through dreams and prophetic vision. The cyclical nature of the Moon and its gravitational influence are also highlighted here, as in situations and relationships shifting and evolving, or perhaps finding yourself inexplicably drawn to something or someone in a game of intrigue. Creativity, psychic ability, and imagination intensify, and your desire to explore the unknown leads to all kinds of new opportunities. Take care, however, that what is hidden from you should not remain so; allow your heightened intuition to serve as a guide through this enchanted night.

## 19 The Sun

The Sun represents the dynamic, vital energy of the true self. The symbolism of this energy is the inner child—that aspect in all of us that embodies innocence, enthusiasm, and joy. With this card comes the opportunity to let your "child" come out and play; creativity, originality, and artistry are all in the spotlight now. This card speaks of mastery in educational and professional arenas, positive growth and material gain, happiness in love and family matters. The Sun brings success to any situation, inspiring all within its influence to new heights of imagination, invention, and achievement. Delight in the possibilities, and let yourself shine!

## 20 Judgment

Judgment is a symbol of transformation and freedom. This card heralds a cry of the spirit, a time to recognize and rise above earthly limitation. You are being asked to re-evaluate your past actions, your present position, and your future desires, and make the changes necessary to accommodate a new spiritual awareness. The challenges have been accepted and squarely faced; enlightenment follows, as well as a heightened ability to access personal power and enhance your everyday life. This card serves as a wake-up call, a reminder of who you are, a message to follow your own conscience and intuition, and to really live rather than simply exist.

## 21 The World

The World is a symbol of completion. With this card you see the whole picture, a synthesis of all the elements required to create the total vision. The World carries a message of mastery, maturity, and the successful outcome of a personal journey or cycle of events. Lessons have been learned, dues have been paid, compromises and conditions have been met. Now comes reward and celebration, the acknowledgment of having achieved what you set out to achieve and having grown and bettered yourself in the process.

# EIGHT

# The Minor Arcana

## Wands

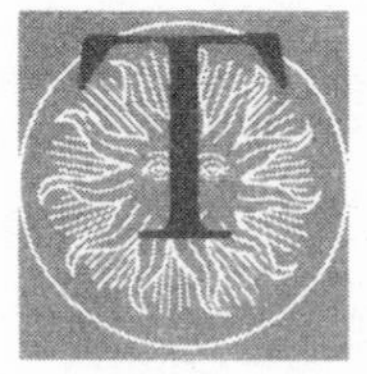

The suit of Wands rules the spiritual realm, where passion, creativity, life force, and desire hold court in a torch-lit palace. Fire is the essential element in this kingdom—a landscape of bright desert plains, fields in the heat of high summer, dragons' lairs and lions' dens, Gypsy camps ringed with wind-blown lanterns and blazing bonfires. Accordingly, the three fire signs of the Zodiac (Aries, Leo, and Sagittarius) are most associated with the suit of Wands, and, for me, the season of Summer and the direction South.

The characters and experiences found in this suit are equally fiery. Its people are warriors—animated, instinctual, willful, motivated toward Spirit and self-actualization. Things move quickly in this place, at times, perhaps, too quickly—even at rest, the Wands are sparking and fizzing with constant energy. The challenges that come with this suit are restlessness, aggression, rebellion, and unfocused ambition; the rewards are personal power, spiritual union, creative and sexual expression, and magic of every kind.

## Ace of Wands

The Ace of Wands is a card of aspiration and desire. This is energy at its peak, a surge of passion and purpose, forged with spirit. Initiation, new projects, enlightenment, bliss; with this card you experience tremendous creative force, a rush of enthusiasm impossible to suppress. It is a comet, streaking across an August sky, the bright, fevered instinct of the chase, lovers reaching climax. Like these, this explosion of power and energy cannot last—it must be focused and savored while it exists.

## Two of wands

The Two of Wands symbolizes independence and dominion. Here you stand at the crest of an experience, having reached this place as a result of your own strength and decision making. From this vantage point the view is endless, and many possible futures lie before you, each with a clearly marked path and potential. With this card you find a wealth of resources available to you and the self-confidence and determination required to utilize them. This is a peaceful interval, a moment of relaxation and review before merrily continuing your journey.

## Three of Wands

The Three of Wands represents opportunity. There is tremendous potential inherent in this card's synthesis of heart, mind, and spirit. From the heart comes hunger and ambition; from the mind, direction and will; from the spirit, the fire and passion necessary to manifest whatever is desired. Life takes on an expressive, childlike quality now, and kindred spirits are everywhere, drawn by the nature of your energy. Collaboration, shared responsibility, integrity, and support for any endeavor you wish to undertake are all hallmarks of this magical card.

## four of wands

The Four of Wands is a symbol of completion. This is a ceremonious card, depicting the security and comfort one can create through virtue, passion, and purpose. Here is the celebration of the harvest, the feasts of Lammas, a wedding procession through garland-draped streets. There is a sense of camaraderie and mutual satisfaction with this card, of success as a result of effort well expended. Enjoy this experience of fulfillment and honor the path that brought you here, as well as those who have traveled alongside you.

## Five of Wands

The Five of Wands symbolizes competition. Here, the fiery nature of this suit reaches a fever pitch, the energy unfocused and in excess. Conflict can result, with another or within yourself, as in the spiritual nature versus the physical, or the head versus the heart. Impasse is likely, with both factions equally strong, equally stubborn regarding their position, and equally blind to the insight and worth of their opponent. If they can lay down their judgment and remove the armor of their egos, in combination, rather than in confrontation, these warring nations can prove a potent force when directed toward a common goal. Cooperation is the key.

## six of wands

The Six of Wands is a card of victory. Here is the warrior returning home from the battle, having triumphed over great adversity. In celebration of his success, the evening fires will be lit and stories will be told of the struggle so that all might learn from the warrior's experience. With this card comes a sense of renewed energy and a chance to revel in your accomplishments, the opportunity to take great strides in your desired direction. This is the time to "fight the good fight"—and, as is always the case when honor and integrity prevail, you will emerge victorious.

## seven of wands

The Seven of Wands represents courage. This is the moment to stand your ground, to accept the challenge of whatever lies before you. This card does not denote confrontation; rather, it represents an inward strength and power that comes with the conviction of your own righteousness. Here, you defend your beliefs without being defensive. You find the support you need and stand firm with it, whether it be a wall, a friend, or a personal vision. It is a time for heroes, and you rise to the call without question and without compromise.

## Eight of Wands

The Eight of Wands is a card of action. This is a time of swift movement, channels of communication opening wide, and the unfettered exchange of pure energy. There is a dizzying aspect to this card. Things will speed up and change at a moment's notice, and choices and options abound. Now is the time to send messages, make contacts, act on wishes and dreams and ideas. Others will see you in a brighter light and respond; love and creativity are electrified. Here is a Gypsy carnival at midnight, Summer Solstice, and the fires of Yule igniting all at once. Reach for the stars!

## Nine of Wands

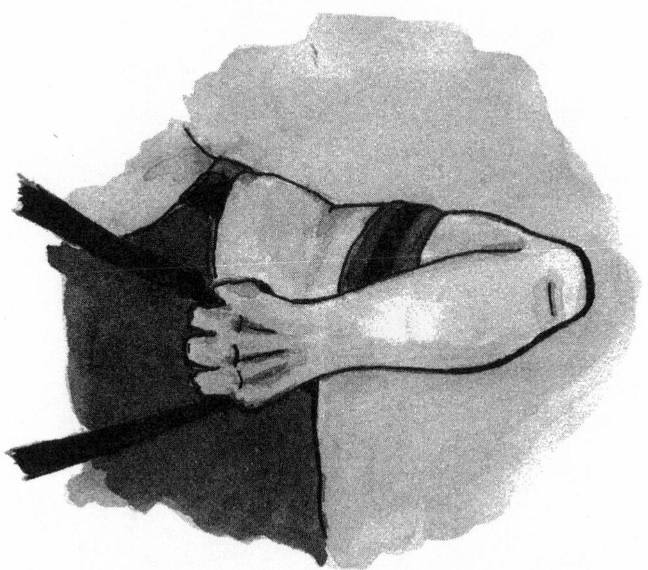

The Nine of Wands is symbolic of strength. This card finds you standing firm, having earned your position through the lessons and challenges of the previous Wands. This is a time for tremendous physical and mental discipline, as well as spiritual focus and connection. Your self-confidence is high, and you direct your energy with accuracy and effect. Here is the warrior preparing to enter the tournament field, confident in his power and prowess, welcoming the chance to prove his might in a show of arms. Challenge becomes a thing to anticipate rather than avoid; with this Nine, you face the future unafraid.

## Ten of wands

The Ten of Wands is a card of responsibility. At times viewed as burdensome or oppressive, this card bears the message of hard work and perseverance, for what you have taken on is not easy. You may have overcommitted yourself on some task or feel you are carrying the sole weight of an overwhelming situation. Ask yourself if your ego is helping to create this predicament, or if it is simply a lack of options; then define what is absolutely essential to the goal and seek assistance where appropriate so your own energies can be focused for the greatest good.

## princess of wands

The Princess of Wands is a delightful, impulsive creature. Her energy and enthusiasm are contagious, proving an inspiration to even the most reserved of people. Her sense of humor is also catching and often mischievous—she is the one who turns the caged tiger loose in the royal gardens on a lark, who steals into the palace kitchen at midnight for an impromptu supper, playing hide-and-seek with the surly tower guards. Her temper is as quick to flame as her whimsy, and her ideas often come and go just as quickly, for she lacks the maturity and experience necessary to bring them to fruition. Opportunities, news, and revelations surround this fiery child—she will awaken you to the spontaneous and creative spirit of life and provide a fearless sense of adventure.

## prince of wands

The Prince of Wands is the adventurer. Courageous and valiant, he plays with risk as if at a game and charges into the unknown with the bearing and confidence of a warrior. Often unpredictable, his competitive, restless nature drives him to seek action and change. He is the first to face down the dragon, storm the battlements to rescue the maiden fair, or carry the flag of his kingdom into uncharted lands. To his friends and loved ones he is a champion, loyal and passionate; to those unaccustomed to or threatened by his fire, he can appear arrogant or self-serving. This Prince will undoubtedly infuse your life with enthusiasm and ambition, possibly inciting you to a change of residence or career.

## Queen of Wands

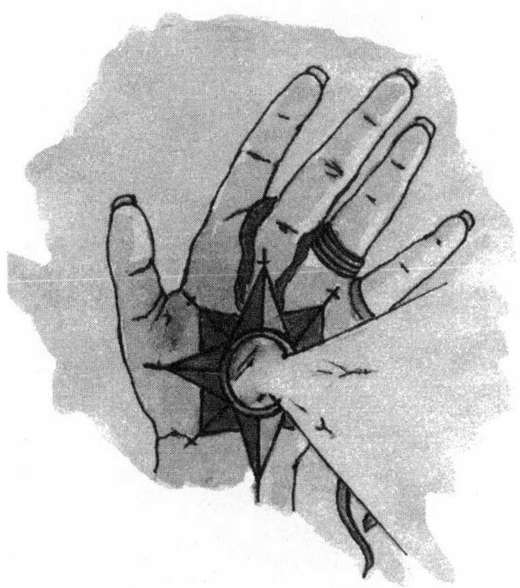

The Queen of Wands is a woman of passion and intensity who can command attention with a single word or glance. People are drawn to her almost magically, as her confident nature puts her in the center of every experience. Integrity is her hallmark, and her creative and visionary qualities move others to seek her out for advice and inspiration. She is the one who champions the hunt, oversees the preparations for the celebratory feast, and then charms the contending royalty. Always striving for self-knowledge and actualization, this Queen can at times become impatient and sharp with those she deems narrow-minded. Magnetic, willful, she will inspire you to revel in your imagination and always speak your truth.

## King of wands

The King of Wands is the visionary. The uncontested master of his personal domain, he is a generous and decisive leader, comfortable in the strength of his convictions. His manner is both honest and charismatic, inspiring respect and admiration in most, and intimidation in others. He is the definitive elder of the pride, battle-scarred, lying in the sun after the hunt, arrogant yet accessible and loving to his young. This King is not afraid to take action, to protect and defend the honor of those closest to him, and he finds his greatest reward in the commission of service. Dynamic, noble, he will empower you to approach any situation with mastery and courage.

# NINE

# The Minor Arcana

## Cups

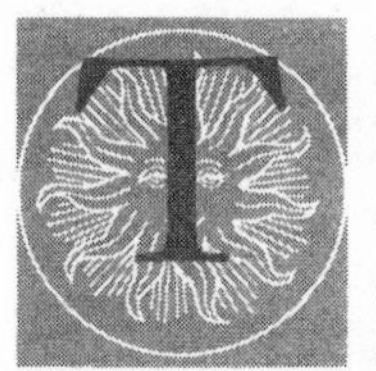

The suit of Cups is all about feeling. Love, romance, intuition, dreams—this watery realm is a magical fantasy of alabaster palaces and mother-of-pearl streets, dolphins swimming in deep green lagoons, carved marble fountains, sparkling streams, and ocean waves crashing on crystalline shores. The three water signs of the Zodiac (Pisces, Cancer, and Scorpio) are linked to the suit of Cups, and, for me, the season of Spring and the direction West.

The inhabitants of this fanciful kingdom are artists, healers, poets, and lovers, immersed in creative pursuits, family and partnership issues, and affairs of the heart. The line between fantasy and reality can blur whenever Cups are involved—the depth and intensity of feeling in this suit calls for the staunchest intellect to drop arms and fall head over heels into emotion. The challenges to be faced with this suit are disillusionment, indulgence, moodiness, and addiction; the rewards are beauty, contentment, emotional and creative fulfillment, and joy.

## Ace of Cups

The Ace of Cups is a card of true love and emotion. This is a heart that is full and passionate but as yet unexpressed, content for the moment simply to feel. Life becomes infused with a sense of joy and anticipation, as if at any moment you might be offered a gift or some rare opportunity. Here are furtive glances and a stolen kiss, a bouquet of flowers left in secret on a porch step, an expectant mother feeling the child within her move for the first time. With this card comes the chance to experience the beginnings of love and all that it promises; the awakening of creative energy and ideas; the possibility and wonder engaged in all matters of the heart.

## Two of Cups

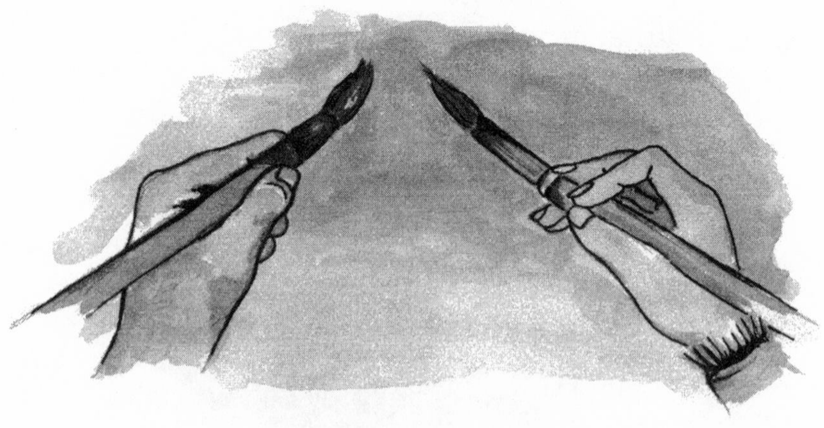

The Two of Cups is a card of romance. The focus here is on partnership and a mutual exchange of energy and positive emotion. Here is creative interplay, the spontaneous invention of two artists meeting beside an empty canvas, brushes in hand. The emotional framework is one of balance and equality. This is the mystical meeting of two kindred spirits, a union that magically blends heart, mind, body, and soul. With this card you experience an opportunity to give and receive love, to connect with another at the deepest level possible and create a common future. Whether of a romantic, familial, or professional nature, this is truly a relationship of "soulmates."

## Three of Cups

The Three of Cups is a card of celebration. The energy here is contagious, the mood one of spontaneous joy and merriment. There is nothing shy or secretive about this card—engagements are announced, festivals are held, babies are named and baptized. Here is opening night at the theatre or the feasts of Beltane, with ribbons and flowers and music 'til dawn. With this Three, expect to be radiant, creative, and, especially, outgoing; opportunities to participate in happy events will be numerous, and supportive and inspirational friends and occasions abound.

## Four of Cups

The Four of Cups symbolizes a time of re-evaluation. Emotional situations of late have lost their appeal; it feels as if a spell has been broken, or perhaps there was never enchantment to begin with. Here, the frog prince returns to his lily pad, and the magic carpet remains in the palace hallway, growing foot-worn and threadbare. With this card you may experience boredom, disillusionment, or unfulfilled expectations. Uncomfortable as it may be, this time can prove a gift, allowing you to retrace your steps, to look carefully at your personal value system, and decide what needs to change in order to have what you desire.

## Five of Cups

The Five of Cups heralds a time of emotional vulnerability, possibly through the loss of something dear to you or as a result of being disappointed in love. The message of this card is to look for the silver lining. A storm is passing, leaving you shaken, but standing, in its wake. Here is a chance to see very clearly what has occurred and to shift the face of future situations by being aware of the roles you have played in the past. There is always opportunity in adversity, and this card beckons you to move to higher ground and review this experience with compassion and understanding and to look on tomorrow with hope rather than despair.

## six of cups

The Six of Cups depicts the innocence and joy of childhood. Here is the candor and sweetness of summer afternoons in a tree house, rainy days spent in the attic fending off dragons and evil spells, a secret pledge between best friends never to grow up or apart. Time slows, and life and love become simple and undemanding. With this card you experience an opportunity to revive those childlike feelings, to create ease and rapport with yourself and others, and to relive the memory and emotion of gentler days.

## Seven of Cups

The Seven of Cups is a card of fantasy and inspiration. Here is a flood of creative energy and ideas, at times overwhelming, and the challenge lies in expressing rather than drowning in them. This card represents spiritual enlightenment in the form of visions or prophetic dreams, heightened psychic abilities, and inspired visualizations. This Seven can also depict the challenge of overcoming addiction or emotional excess and finding more constructive ways to utilize your thoughts and energies. Your imagination can either be your ally or your enemy; you have the opportunity to choose which it shall be.

## Eight of Cups

The Eight of Cups is a card of sacrifice. This Eight can symbolize a moment of emptiness and emotional exhaustion, the result of continuously giving your energy away to others. You have become the sacrifice here. Now it is time to withdraw from situations or relationships in which you have been the main source of strength and tend to your own needs. With this card comes an opportunity to recognize your patterns of excess caregiving, to balance your own needs with the needs of others, and to honor your emotional boundaries.

## Nine of Cups

The Nine of Cups is a card of fulfillment. This is a time of fairy-tale anticipation, of dreams coming true, both within yourself and in your outer world. Whatever your heart desires will come to pass with this card. You get to catch a falling star, find a genie's lamp, and cast a magic pebble into the sea. Know that this streak of good fortune is deserved and that tapping into the flow of Universal abundance is everyone's birthright. Let no shadows of fear or guilt darken your sense of delight. Just make sure that what you wish for is truly in your best interest, for you will likely get it when this Nine appears!

## Ten of Cups

The Ten of Cups represents success. There is a deep sense of personal satisfaction with this card to experience and savor in all areas of your life. It is a time for celebration, for acknowledging your spiritual connection with family and friends, for basking in the glow of a life lived well. Here you receive recognition for goals already attained and the support and inspiration to work toward your future desires. The admiration and respect of your peers, the warmth of enduring love, and the security and contentment of lasting achievement are all gifts of this wonderful card and the result of your own right work. Bravo!

## Princess of Cups

A fey and charming child, the Princess of Cups lives with her devoted family in a beautiful kingdom by the sea. Her dreamy, poetic nature and sense of fancy lead her to spend many hours gathering seashells and ribbons and pink glass beads, which she uses to fashion intricate talismans of love and romance. At times impressionable and naïve, often deeply affected by the words or deeds of others, this emotional Princess is nonetheless willing at any moment to bandage a broken wing, pick the brightest, freshest flowers for the palace sickroom, or spin the perfect tale to banish the shadows of a nightmare. Gentle and kind, she will be the first to impart news of a romantic or creative nature, and her messages always inspire hope and delight.

## prince of cups

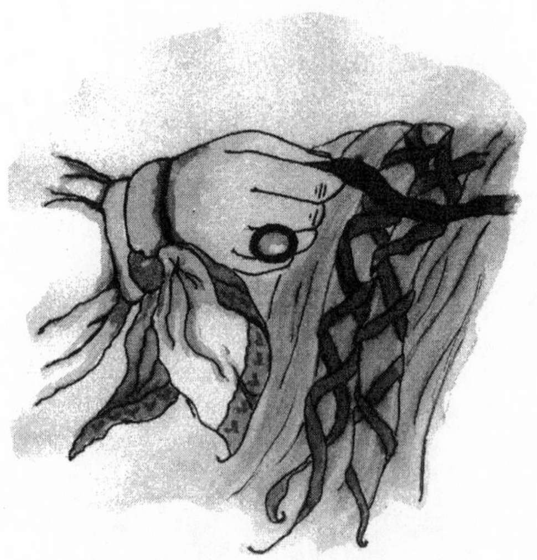

The Prince of Cups is the lover. Romantic and sensitive, he carries the flag of true chivalry and holds his heart in his hand for all to see. Gifted with an expressive, emotional nature, he finds delight in music and the arts, and he in turn can hold others spellbound with his own talents and charm. His idealism and passion can send him spinning off on a gallant's quest, wearing the kerchief of his most recent beloved tied with the ribbons of the broken hearts he has left behind. It's not that he is deliberately callow or deceitful; in fact, he often proves to be the truest friend one could ever know. But when it comes to affairs of the heart, this Prince is truly in love with love alone.

## Queen of Cups

The Queen of Cups is the storybook empress. Gentle, loving, kind, she not only provides for the needs and comforts of her own family but sees to the welfare of all in the kingdom. She is a faithful and devoted wife, offering wise counsel and quiet support to the King and his ministry. Imaginative, empathetic, she nurtures the dreams and desires of all closest to her, as well as her own. Her very touch can be dramatically healing, moving others to seek her out for assistance and care, which she tirelessly gives. At times her maternal instincts can become overbearing, and she must be on guard against her own emotional insecurities. This generous and good-natured woman will inspire you to help those less fortunate than yourself and to connect more deeply with your own intuitive and nurturing aspects.

## King of Cups

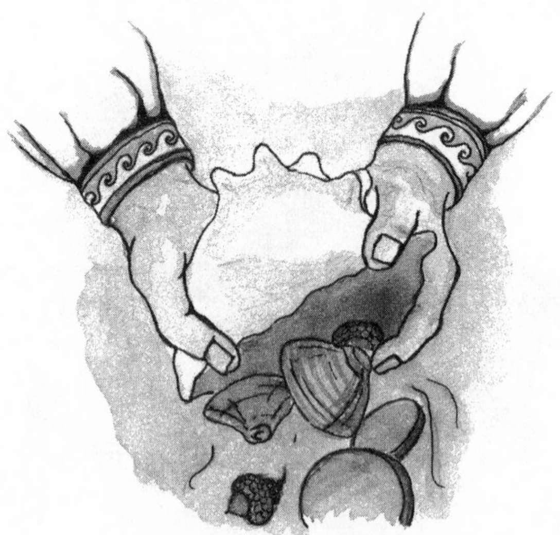

The King of Cups is a charitable ruler who treats all of his subjects with the same care and respect he affords his own family. He is a quiet-tempered man, at ease in the role of husband and father as well as sovereign. A keen eye for beauty and a flair for drama and the arts prove him a champion of style and elegance. His easy manner and philosophical approach inspire many to seek his counsel, and he imparts advice and creative solutions with aplomb. However, his calm demeanor protects a depth of intense emotion, and this King can be roused to great passion if what he loves is harmed or threatened in any way. This gracious and benevolent King can impart to you the wisdom of emotional mastery and expression.

# TEN

# The Minor Arcana

## pentacles

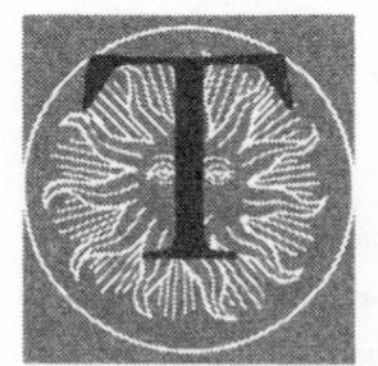

he suit of Pentacles governs the physical world. Money, health, worldly possessions, and the manifestation of ideas and goals in tangible form are all elemental components of the earth kingdom. The castles and townships found in this land are built of the finest natural materials by master craftsmen; the hills and forests surrounding are lush and verdant. The gardens in the square are manicured riots of green, and fat sheep and sturdy dray horses graze in clover-thick fields. The three earth signs of the Zodiac (Taurus, Virgo, and Capricorn) are connected to the suit of Pentacles, and, for me, the season of Autumn and the direction North.

The people of this suit are as stable and as solid as their environment. They are strong, sensual, practical, and wise, well versed in business, medicine, and agriculture. They work hard, pacing themselves to the rhythms of their labors, yet they know well how to relax and revel in their many accomplishments. The challenges of this suit can be found in materialism, selfishness, possessiveness, or rigidity; the rewards are attainment, security, comfort, and earthly pleasures.

## Ace of pentacles

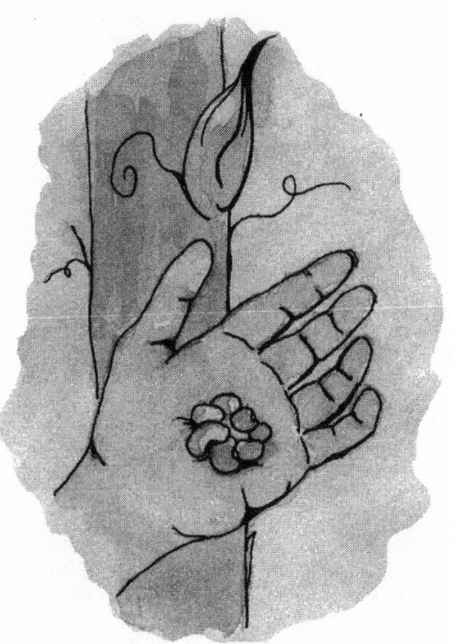

The Ace of Pentacles symbolizes reward. Any project or situation associated with this card is assured a successful, prosperous outcome. Like seedlings in a well-tended garden, new and promising financial opportunities take root, opening you to a dynamic flow of energy and resource. Gifts of money or practical advice come your way as well as a general sense of security and well-being. Do not take this wellspring of gain for granted, however; this card represents but a step in the evolutionary journey, which must include recession as well as flow.

## Two of pentacles

The Two of Pentacles is a symbol of change. This card brings an awareness of the cyclical nature of all things, particularly the material and physical worlds. Just as the Earth and her seasons shift and evolve, so does the energy source we know as money. Maintaining balance and seeking direction, facing decisions and welcoming opportunities, prioritizing and conserving resources are all indicated here. The message is to be flexible and see change as an opportunity for growth and to learn from the changes and cycles you have already endured.

## Three of Pentacles

The Three of Pentacles represents work. Here you experience the development of ideas and the necessary discipline and tenacity to carry them through, as well as the formation of alliances with kindred souls who can assist you in moving toward your goal. As a result, you will see the outgrowth of your efforts and enjoy the satisfaction of shared achievements with friends and coworkers. You may encounter brambles and thorns, rocks or mountains as you toil, but each obstacle you overcome renews your sense of focus and commitment for the future.

## four of pentacles

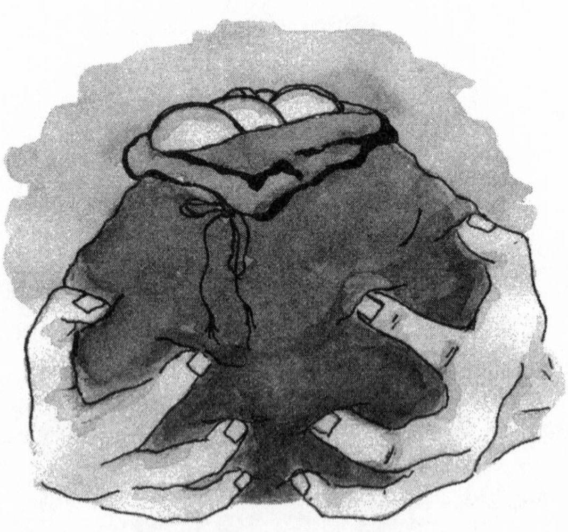

The Four of Pentacles contains a message regarding wealth and ownership. This card may signal a time of increased financial and material worth and power, but you need to take care that this accumulation does not decrease your own self-worth. Greed, selfishness, and suspicion are highlighted here, not only in the material realm but in the personal as well. Consider the miser, counting stacks of gold each night in his dark and drafty castle, miserable and alone. Who or what are you fighting to possess? Learn to accept the flow of wealth into your life and know that you are worthy of it. Value and integrity are the real riches; if you are truly self-possessed, you can never be poor.

## Five of pentacles

The Five of Pentacles is a card of concern and adversity. Issues of health or finances may be creating anxiety; a storm front appears to be moving in and the coming darkness seems overwhelming. With this Five you are challenged to re-create your reality, to consider how your perceptions of any situation affect your reaction, to find the lantern glowing through the hurricane. In times of struggle it is essential to conserve your energy, to focus on the next immediate step through the darkness rather than the lightning and thunder on the far horizon. If you keep your thoughts in the present, and for the moment turn off the path of your imagination, you will likely find the winds of change blowing your worst possible future clean away, leaving clear skies and fresh opportunity in its wake.

## six of pentacles

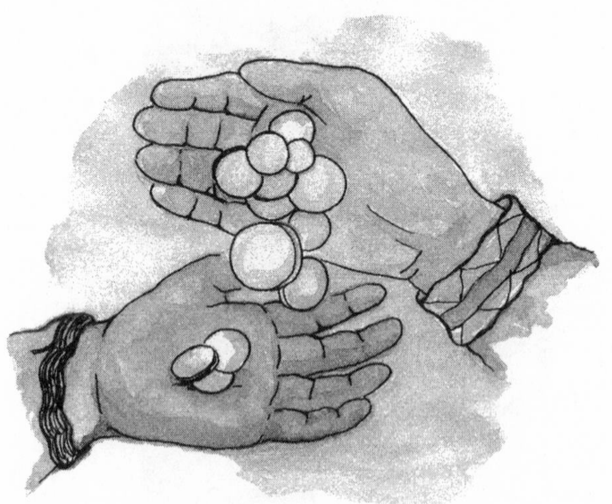

The Six of Pentacles celebrates the nature of generosity. This is a card of bounty, of material and physical comforts. It represents a time to experience the flow of abundance through yourself and others. Here you find your needs met above and beyond expectation; money and other resources come your way through unforeseen channels. With this Six you discover your own charitable nature as well and experience the joy of sharing your good fortune with those who need it. To give, without expectation of return, will make you rich indeed.

## seven of pentacles

The Seven of Pentacles can signify a situation that requires patience. There is an indication of tremendous effort on your part and frustration at not seeing the fruits of your labor born as quickly as you desire. Worry, fear of failure, doubt, and haste can all be elements of this Seven. The remedy is not to pull the seedlings from the ground to see if they have taken root; but rather, to stand by stoically and trust that they will show themselves of their own good nature and accord.

## eight of pentacles

The Eight of Pentacles represents a foundation built of your own wisdom and experience. This card signifies growth and careful productivity, paying attention to detail, being disciplined and well prepared. There is a strong sense of craftsmanship and ability with this card; here you stand before the canvas, marveling at the colors and shadows and lines you have already captured, envisioning the final masterpiece and the steps that remain to its ultimate completion. With this Eight you experience the satisfaction of creating for your future and the knowledge that you've done it well.

## Nine of Pentacles

The Nine of Pentacles represents abundance. Imagine Eden in full bloom, vines and branches heavy with fruit, flowers lush and fragrant. This is a card of earthly pleasures, of recognizing your worth, of living in comfort. There could be an inheritance, a settlement, or winnings of some kind, and great financial increase is likely. Money is not the only gain with this Nine, however; creativity, love, and well-being are all enhanced. This is a time to savor your riches, to trust that this financial independence and freedom is reward for hard work done well. Above all, recognize that you deserve it!

## Ten of pentacles

The Ten of Pentacles signifies wealth and security. The situation depicted by this card is graced with good fortune and protection, built upon a foundation of tradition, wisdom, and heritage. Wise investments, retirement, and material comfort founded upon past endeavors are all possibilities here. With this Ten you are surrounded by supportive and loving kin, secure in your material and financial future, and grateful for the past and all that has led to this present position. The peace and assurance you find with this card becomes a stronghold from which all your dreams can safely take flight and to which each adventure happily returns you.

## princess of pentacles

Beneath a sturdy oak tree near the castle gate sits the Princess of Pentacles, her pockets full of acorns and seeds, her small nose hidden in a book. She is a quiet, down-to-earth, sensible child who loves literature and numbers and all the natural world. She is known throughout the kingdom for her reliable, hard-working nature, always ready to pitch in when a garden needs tending or a lamb is struggling to be born. Her contemplative, cautious temperament leads some to believe her dull or slow-witted, and at times she can appear overprotective of money or personal possessions. Yet her careful deliberation and studious manner prove a valuable asset in any practical situation. This Princess will likely bring news of the business or material worlds and remind you of the importance of study and enterprise.

## prince of pentacles

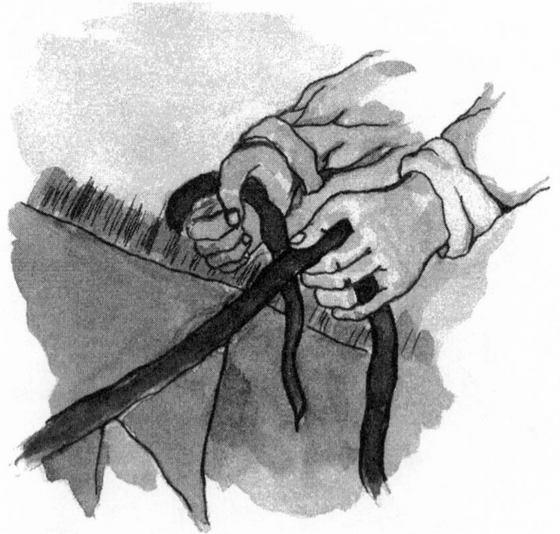

The Prince of Pentacles is the guardian. A serious, responsible young man who understands the rhythms of the Earth and the animals, he strives to honor and protect all in his domain. His love of Nature and the outdoors often carries him far from the confines of castle walls, into the verdant forests and foothills at the edge of the kingdom; his skill in the hunt and his knowledge of plant life assure his family is well fed upon his return. Patient, persistent, at times even stubborn in his approach, this Prince sees to the physical and mundane aspects of daily life with humor and a lusty spirit. His steadfast and trustworthy nature will inspire you to strive for your own goals with a similar energy and to concentrate on the details of the task at hand.

## Queen of pentacles

The Queen of Pentacles is a calm and practical woman, interested in the land and its right management and the welfare of all its inhabitants. With an eye for organization and an uncanny ability to seek out and unify supporting factions, this Queen is often found spearheading events to promote another's talents or some worthwhile environmental cause. Attention to detail and a shrewd business sense combined with a charitable nature lead others to seek her out for guidance and favor. She champions financial security and comfort and cherishes her family above all else. Let her inspire you to care for the Earth and those around you and to use your talents to support and nurture all.

## King of pentacles

The King of Pentacles is a paragon of royalty, the powerful father figure who rules all in his empire with honesty, virtue, and fairness. Uncompromising in his self-discipline, this King has built his fortunes through wise dealings and sound investments, hard work and honorable intent. Tradition is his hallmark; conscience, his seal; security, his principle and reward. From his position of financial success and material satisfaction, he is able to focus his considerable energy on guiding and supporting those around him. There are some who would consider him too conventional or unprogressive in his views; others find his conservative and steadfast manner a comfort and an inspiration. This King will impart dependable advice or financial assistance, guide you to important contacts, and above all, fortify your own sense of responsibility and potential.

## ELEVEN

# The Minor Arcana
## Swords

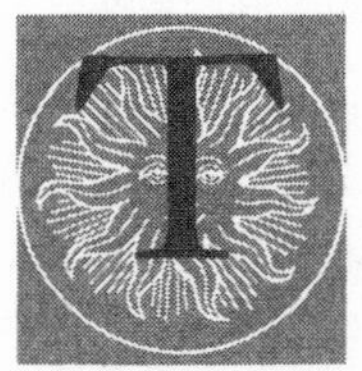

The suit of Swords rules the kingdom of air. This is the intellectual realm, a world of reason, logic, communication, and truth. Towering mountain peaks and angled cliffs dominate the landscape; campaniles and castle towers mark the boundary of cities against stone. Eagles ride the updrafts of icy winds, soaring far above snowdrifts and caverns of crystal; white wolves gather in keen-eyed silence at dusk in the silvery woods. The three air signs of the Zodiac (Gemini, Libra, and Aquarius) are affiliated with the suit of Swords, and, for me, the season of Winter, and the direction East.

The people of this sharp and somewhat austere land are quick witted and clever, brilliant arbitrators, known for a particular mastery of law and languages. In the kingdom of Swords, literature, psychology, and political intrigue are favorite pursuits; no choice is made without careful deliberation, for judgment and intent are prized above all. The challenges of this suit can appear as self-criticism, being overly analytical, a lack of compassion or empathy, and depression; the rewards are objectivity, individuality, intelligence, and honesty.

## Ace of swords

The Ace of Swords symbolizes clarity. There is tremendous intellectual energy and purpose with this Ace; doubt and uncertainty are cut away, revealing fresh ideas and the skill and understanding necessary to carry them out. There is also a message within this card regarding truth: Know and speak your own truth while accepting and honoring another's. This is the card of the knight who champions the Queen, Percival at King Arthur's court, the power of Excalibur lodged in stone. Only the pure of heart and mind can wield this sword—find your truth and your purpose and you can conquer any adversity.

## Two of Swords

The Two of Swords represents balance. This card heralds a time of peace following conflict or confusion, a mental sanctuary in which to reflect on what has transpired and to contemplate your direction for the future. Perhaps you have faced a difficult decision or a choice that required great evaluation before resolving. Now you can relax and allow things to stabilize, secure in your present position and knowing that you have chosen wisely. The mood of this card is serene, reflecting a clear and positive state of mind. This awareness will serve as sacred space, allowing you the confidence to move forward and the comfort of a shelter to which you can return during life's inevitable storms.

## Three of Swords

The Three of Swords can represent the process of sorrow or grief. Grief is an ego-less state, an experience of loss in which you cannot control the emotional dramas being played out in your mind. Something or someone whom you believed to play a central role in this fantasy has proved untrue. Lack of focus, disappointment, bitterness, and mistrust are all symptoms of your awakening to the reality of this situation. Healing comes when you accept and allow the grieving process to happen, when you step across your dark mental landscape and release the quixotic expectations that helped create the scenario in the first place.

## four of swords

The Four of Swords symbolizes seclusion and retreat. This card may find you calling an emotional truce with yourself, creating a grounded, meditative state in which to recoup lost energy. The external chaos of life continues to rage all around you, but with your emotional and mental boundaries firmly established, you can remain calm and centered. Recovery, rest, self-reflection, insight; this Four represents the need for withdrawal and solitude for the purpose of healing one's mind and spirit.

## Five of Swords

The Five of Swords represents the need to defeat outmoded patterns of thought or behavior. Negative belief structures, judgmental attitudes, and destructive mind games are the adversaries here; any mental process that no longer serves you must be acknowledged, understood, and conquered. This is the card of the dragon slayer—one who charges forth, determined and self-directed, who knows his quarry as well as himself. One must understand the beast before it can be vanquished.

## six of swords

The Six of Swords is a symbol of passage. This card represents a change for the better, crossing over from struggle to serenity. The shift may come following some new awareness or attitude or after a period of confusion and uncertainty. A journey is often indicated by this card. Whether it be a spiritual, emotional, or physical quest, the transition is always toward enlightenment. This Six also points to the cyclical nature of life and the understanding that nothing remains the same forever. So have faith that the storm clouds will pass and the stars will shine out of the darkness once more to guide you on your way.

## seven of swords

The Seven of Swords speaks to the importance of individuality. This card symbolizes opposition and negative outside forces. Removing yourself from these crippling influences and being aware of your own patterns of self-sabotage are vital steps in creating the future you desire. Doubt, restlessness, fear of contradicting the collective mind; all are weapons you must arm yourself against in order to follow your true path. This is the card of the vision quest, of stealing away into the wilderness to find your spiritual voice and live as your soul intended. The world would have you crawl in orthodoxy; you must fly with defiance and true spirit.

## eight of swords

The Eight of Swords signifies restricted energy, feeling trapped or blocked by your own thought processes. Choice made up of too many options and not enough information, interference from outside influence or internal dialogue, being blinded to the greater picture by over-analyzing singular details—this card presents you with an opportunity to clear the web of confusion by simply waiting, calming your mind, and allowing your higher consciousness to shed light on the solution. The answer you seek will come with composure not coercion.

## Nine of Swords

The Nine of Swords is symbolic of the process of self-censure and judgment. This card represents the nightmare visuals created by an overactive, theatrical imagination, riding shotgun with a critical mind. *Should haves, what ifs,* worst-case scenarios—all are painted on the canvas of your inner eye with impossible color and clarity. The message here is, Take control of your mental process. Grab the reins, slow the coach, toss away the brushes and the paint box. Focus your thoughts on your victories and attributes and reconnect to your spiritual center—and send your "critic" out for a long lunch.

## Ten of swords

The Ten of Swords represents the experience of being mentally and emotionally overwhelmed. This card brings an unbalanced phase, relationship, or situation to an end, possibly throwing you even further off-balance as a result of having held on long past an appropriate finale. Exhaustion brought on by this particular set of circumstances, followed by the fear of change, feelings of loss and regret all create a convincing emotional portrait of devastation. But depression is a symptom, not a disease—now is the moment to let go and allow time and spirit to heal the wounds of this important struggle.

## Princess of Swords

High in the castle tower waits the spirited Princess of Swords, leaning from the battlements, spyglass in hand, an expression of delighted anticipation on her slender face. She is positive that, somewhere on the castle grounds, someone is doing something fascinating. Such is the inquisitive nature of this intriguing and at times exasperating child. Ideas and activity captivate her, and her mind is constantly awhirl with news and information often gleaned from unusual sources. Her curious manner and love of exposition lead many to label her a gossip; those closest to her know her as a witty, intelligent girl who is honest and clever, but whose quick mind can at times be outpaced by her even quicker tongue. This bright Princess will likely surprise you with unexpected news, innovative concepts, or unforeseen events.

## prince of swords

The Prince of Swords is the truthsayer. Charismatic and outspoken, this young man rides out into the world with righteous and battle-ready zeal. Noted for his clever, inventive speech and philosophical viewpoints, this Prince is quick to react to opposition and will jump at the chance to engage his opponent in a verbal contest of wills. His mercurial nature and a tendency toward imprudence lead some to believe him thoughtless and rash; those who know him well, however, are drawn by his admirable courage, and his tireless pursuit of justice. He will no doubt provoke all kinds of movement in your life, in the form of events, people, and ideas, and encourage you to sharpen your own communication skills.

## Queen of swords

The Queen of Swords is a complex, intelligent woman, with a voice like spun silk and eyes like tempered steel. She spends her days engaged in intellectual pursuits, writing and researching, and being an authority on numerous subjects; she can lecture and instruct on many levels. At times this Queen can seem sharp and domineering, if only to get her ideas across, but she is also known throughout the kingdom as a wise, impartial counselor who seeks to influence others toward positive changes. Bold and independent, she will motivate you to empower your mind, triumph over your challenges, and achieve personal liberation.

## King of Swords

The stately King of Swords presides over his empire with wisdom and modest aplomb. Mental stimulation is his lifeblood; he constantly seeks out opportunity to exercise his analytical and psychological strengths. Like his Queen he is highly educated, well versed in a myriad of subjects, and a brilliant arbitrator, benefiting others with his considerable authority. His refined, rational manner and powerful intellect lead some to consider him cold and emotionally distant, yet he is just and diplomatic with all his subjects, in any situation. This sage King will advise you to be fair in all your dealings, to seek out mentors and intellectual guides, and to share your own knowledge with others.

# PART III

# Heaven and Earth

# TWELVE

# Spreads, Timelines, and Why the King and Queen Aren't Speaking

## Taking a Reading to the Next Level

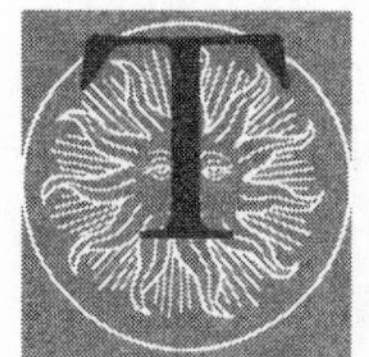

Two knights on horseback face each other across a narrow expanse of ground. One brandishes a weapon, the other offers up a gift in a mailed hand; one mount is steady and quiet in its stance, the other is restless, primed for the charge. Soldiers of fortune, or two champions defending respective kingdoms? Are they poised to fight, or is a treaty in the offing? The answer depends entirely upon the subject of your inquiry and more, of course, upon your instinctual perception of the two warriors.

The relationships between the different cards in a Tarot layout provide yet another fascinating layer of intuitive insight. The interplay of imagery via expression, body language, position, even color, can speak volumes about the issue in question. Your intuitive eye will help define the mood and atmosphere of the answer and, as in the illustration of the contending knights, allow you to determine whether the posturing is truly contentious or purely playful.

In this chapter, we're going to play as well—intuiting timelines through seasonal imagery and working with a few classic Tarot spreads to get a feel for their structure and form. But first, let's take a look at how the images of the cards relate to one another in a layout and see what secrets those liaisons might reveal.

## Family Dynamics

Say you pull the King of Wands and the Queen of Swords side by side in a reading; the King on the left and the Queen on the right, facing away from one another, both wearing regal smiles upon their handsome faces. Depending upon your question, these two might appear right away as dogged opponents pulling in opposite directions, struggling for control of circumstance, their smiles turned to grimaces of lock-jawed determination and will. Or, you might see them instead as strong and loyal allies, standing back to back in a supportive stance, each confident in their own and each other's abilities to handle any situation. Drawn in reverse, so that the King is to the right and the Queen is to the left, eye to eye, they could show up as the knights did—contenders for some royal cause; or, facing each other as partners, building a kingdom of equality and respect.

Sound confusing? Don't let it be. This isn't anything you have to "figure out." Remember—you're looking at the cards in the context of your question and letting your first instinctual reaction set the tone.

Trust me when I tell you that you'll see your mother in the Queen's smiling countenance, if that's appropriate, or sense your own stubborn attachment to a work issue in the King's clenched teeth and iron stance. Allow your intuition to point you in the direction of the appropriate intimations, and the more you work with the cards, the more subtle and exquisite those messages will become.

Following are some key channels of interactive information, found in the relationships between the cards and their images in a layout:

### MOVEMENT

Look for characters in one card heading toward or away from principal images in other cards, for example, a man on horseback in the Six of Wands riding steadily toward a castle in the Ten of Pentacles; the Princess of Swords racing gleefully down a hill, leaving behind a village scene in the Six of Cups; people or animals escaping one another, or joining together, either in cooperation or contest. What do avoidance or complicity have to say within the context of your reading? What about ownership versus abandonment? Trust the intuitive direction this kind of "hit" can give you.

Compare landscapes between cards—does the rocky terrain of one card give way to the gentler hills and rolling pastures of another, or lead you to an even harsher world of crags and granite cliffs? Do the cards in your layout journey from cityscape to countryside, from desert plains to ocean beaches, or does the environment remain similar throughout? Even color can express movement, as angry reds and fiery yellows soothe beneath a wash of blue and lavender, or cold winter grays and silvers warm to the first rose blush of a summer morning. Symbolic movement can illustrate specific, detailed experience or simply clarify an overall attitude of the situation being explored.

### BODY LANGUAGE

An arm outstretched, either in need or in aid, a fist raised in victory or challenge, hands clasped in prayer or consternation, arms crossed in strength or obstinacy—these are all elements of body language that can bring intuitive insight to a reading. In one layout, the Magician might be reaching out to assist the woman in the Nine of Swords; in another, he might appear as though he's handing her a nightmare. The Hermit, lifting his beaming lantern, is either illuminating or exposing the Seven of Swords, depending upon your intuitive perspective.

A gentlewoman in the Nine of Pentacles turns her back to a hurricane, raging across the Tower—in denial of the danger, propelled by the winds, or overcoming an intense but temporary problem? The Lovers dancing naked in the brilliance of a midday Sun might mean being foolishly blinded by the light, potentially burned by the force of the fire, or openly welcoming a new and shining opportunity. Again, trust your intuitive impulse—the energy of the exchange will make itself clear.

### EXPRESSION

Here's where subtlety takes center stage. A smile can be strained or genuine; a frown can appear as disapproval, disquiet, or critical concentration. Sensing the mood of the characters in a layout requires absolute intuitive abandon—sometimes the farmer in the Seven of Pentacles appears frustrated, other times he seems to look upon his labors with satisfaction and pride. The woman in the Two of Swords can seem to you either comforted by, or terrified of, the shimmering blades she wields .... Trust what you feel regarding what you see.

### REPEAT IMAGERY

I find repeated patterns of images in a layout particularly intriguing. Besides the obvious motifs found in the four suits, look for things like roses in the landscape of every card; the sun in several skies or popping up as a carved or painted symbol; significant shapes echoed in architecture or costumes; particular animals or emblems or colors showing up to link each card with the next. Whatever that specific image symbolizes for you is carried throughout the reading and adds a definite touch of coincidental magic to a layout.

### ENERGETIC PLACEMENT

Another symbolic tack you can take is noticing the position of cards according to the energetic placement of masculine/feminine used in ritual. Take our original King versus. Queen pairing on page 182—the King on the left in the feminine position, the Queen on the right in the masculine. This could show up as a challenging aspect, with both characters fighting to prove their standing in opposite courts, or it might feel as though each ruler is well balanced when it comes to their individual yin/yang energies. With positions reversed, their energetic placements would now be "correct," and the interpretation could again go either way—with the King and Queen seemingly comfortable in their respective roles, or feeling trapped by the hierarchy of status and convention.

### INTUITIVE PLACEMENT

As I mentioned earlier, I throw cards on the table—and I do mean that *literally*. I toss them wherever I feel like they should go, and sometimes I rearrange them once they've landed. The whole time I'm tossing, I'm usually talking (which I'm certain, seeing as you've come this far, is not at all hard to imagine), so I'm not *thinking* about where the cards are ending up. I'm just tossing. Sometimes I'm guided to throw four or five; sometimes I stop at a dozen or more. (Me and the faeries—we're *tight*.) Once the cards are down, part of the intrigue is to see who got paired with whom; who or what's above or below or behind the rest; if anybody's ganging up, or someone's left standing alone. This method offers fascinating insights into attitude, personality, and environment—issues of domination and submission, passivity and aggression, secrecy and truth, camaraderie and isolation. It also definitely requires that you silence our good friend Doubt, trusting that where you're instinctively guided to drop the cards is the most auspicious place they could possibly be.

### CARD COMBINATIONS

This one's right up there with repeat imagery on the magical-quotient scale. Besides a possible monopoly of Major or Minor Arcana cards in any given layout, pay attention to how many cards of the different suits show up; how many Aces, Tens, Princesses, etc.; a predominance of men versus woman; a majority of reds or golds or purples. Three out of four cards are Pentacles? Whatever the question, a look at the earthy or physical nature of the issue is probably warranted. Two Princesses, a Queen, and our lady of Justice? Check out the feminine perspective. Several Twos on the table? Matters of partnership and balance are most likely at hand, for better or for worse; let your instincts decide and take you down the appropriate speculative path.

Card combos are a one-way ticket to the goose bumps and "eerily obvious messages" I promised you a couple of chapters ago. One of my favorite experiences happened during a reading about a client's young daughter—an extraordinary little soul, with huge blue eyes and a wisdom and spirit so far beyond her years it's sometimes scary. (I've had the pleasure of this young person's company on several occasions, and I'm always waiting for faerie antennae to sprout and wings to unfurl from her shoulders.) Mom wanted to know what her daughter's guides had to say about her. Plenty! I shuffled, let the deck split, plunked down four cards, and began merrily chatting away, one card to the next. When I reached the third card, I stopped, suddenly speechless—a minor miracle in itself. But that was nothing compared to what lay on the table. I had pulled all four of the Aces! An amazing demonstration, not only because of the odds, but because those four cards *totally* confirmed this child's exceptional light and energy. (And called for breaking out the Kleenex box, for *both* Mom and me.)

And recently I did a reading for a friend regarding her strong attraction to a man she'd just met; she wanted to know what the future potential was for their relationship. I pulled the Magician, the High Priestess, and the Two of Cups, in that order. The Magician and the High

Priestess are perfect partners—equal in energy and personal power, one of the two most potent couples in the deck, alongside the Emperor and the Empress. And the Two of Cups, in the *Robin Wood* deck, is a beautiful illustration of a sacred marriage, angelic influence and all. I don't think we could have gotten a more obvious message, and needless to say, my friend was pleased!

## card games

Now, while we're on the subject of magical combinations and interactive psychic info, I'd like to introduce you to the Queen Mother of all interactive opportunity—a little something I like to call "Dueling Tarot." Picture this:

You and one or more of your friends (one of you is the querent), each armed with a deck (different decks are *really* fun!), pulling the same number of cards for the same question, and each interpreting your own and each other's cards, individually and collectively. Incredible amounts of information come pouring through, with everyone's perspective sparking everyone else's, leading to deeper and deeper exploration. Not to mention the intense psychic energy a group of spiritually open friends can generate. Talk about movement and body language!

Watch for the same card showing up from several decks, identical symbols appearing repeatedly, or combinations of numbers too obvious to be mere coincidence. What are the chances of two people, using two separate decks comprised of seventy-eight well-shuffled cards, pulling the exact same three cards, at the same time, in the exact same order? A pre-reading drum ritual, a very spirited friend, incense, candles, and an

August Full Moon all contributed to one of the wildest Dueling card moments I've ever experienced.

A slightly less intense but equally effective version of the Duel is flying solo, using several different decks to do one reading. Ask your question and pull three cards from each deck, lay them out, interpret each layout individually, and then pool the information. Or, try pulling one card from several different decks, lay them out together, and interpret. This is where the interplay between the cards becomes especially fascinating, with the combination of different artists and mediums, even the size of the different cards having merit.

I always do one of these "hodgepodge" spreads with my students at the end of each Tarot workshop, with a volunteer from the class as the querent. After the question is asked, everyone pulls a card from their deck of choice, lays it on the table with everyone else's, and the high jinks begin. Sometimes there are thirty or more cards in the lineup! Watercolors go to war with photo montages, Priestesses dance with peasants and angels, and dragons come face to face with warriors and modern-day flying machines. At first, the barrage of images can seem a bit daunting, but inevitably everyone loosens up and finds that, much like the students themselves, this eclectic tangle of color and symbolism has a whole lot in common and a whole lot to share. And so, in turn, do they.

## To Everything There Is a Timeline. . . .

Second only to the card definitions on the anticipation scale, timelines provide a means of divining approximately *when* something will come to pass. I'm telling you, this can be dangerous territory. Who among us has *not* gone home after a psychic reading and marked their calendars, literally and/or figuratively? Let's have a show of hands, now ... anyone? Anyone? Anyone? (A smile of grim satisfaction.) Thought so. And how many have been righteously disappointed when said calendar pages came and went, along with the prophesied events, as yet unrealized?

Obviously, we've all lived to tell this tale, but before I spill the magic beans here and send you gallivanting off across your Daytimers, indulge me for one quick moment upon my soapbox, won't you? Timelines, like anything else related to divining the future, are not set in stone, but are simply potential, subject to planetary shenanigans, spiritual evolution, and the whims and wiles of the Human condition. Timelines can be astonishingly accurate or completely capricious, depending upon a number of factors, not the least of which is Divine Timing, wherein the calendar belongs to God, not us. And to that I say, *Hallelujah!* anyway!

Estimating the *when* of the *what* is an undeniable part of the magic of a Tarot reading, and more often than not, a useful one; just be flexible and willing to tag the expression "This or Something Better" onto your readings. Better yet, write it on your calendar!

## SPRING, SUMMER, VIRGO, AND SAG

One of the simplest ways to begin working with timelines is via seasons and astrological factors. As we discussed in chapter 6, there are traditional seasonal correspondences attached to the four suits of the Minor Arcana as well as the astrological connections to the elements of earth, air, fire, and water. Here's an exercise I use in class to stretch those boundaries and help you connect on a more energetic level to the Wheel of the Year.

Go through the deck and pull out the Kings, Queens, and Aces of each suit. Starting with the Aces, lay them out side by side and compare their imagery. Let yourself *sense* the cards (there's that New Age thing again!), imagining you were outdoors, perhaps, in a field or by a river's edge, experiencing the energy depicted. Then arrange the Aces by your sense of Spring, Summer, Autumn, and Winter.

Now do the same thing with the Queens, followed by the Kings. Did the order in which you placed the suits change in any of the groupings or stay the same? In most decks, the Aces are pretty simplistic in their imagery, usually depicting a single element of their suit rather than a character in action. With the Kings and Queens, you're considering matters of expression, costuming, scenery, and the like, which can influence your intuitive feel for the seasons.

In an actual reading, of course, you won't be limiting yourself to pulling a chance Ace or Court card to get a timeline. I use these cards in this exercise because in most decks, their imagery tends to be thematic, making the example a bit more obvious. In an actual reading, and particularly when first learning to intuit time and seasons, I suggest you shuffle your deck, ask for a timeline regarding your issue and then pull a single card, exploring its symbolism from an emotional and sensory perspective as you did in the exercise. After you've become more adept, you'll be able to discern time frames from the body of any layout, using the imagery and energy of all the cards pulled.

So what might you look for in terms of seasonal symbology? Terrain can say a lot—a desert plain can represent a summer's drought, or the dry dog-end of the September harvest, when fields are shorn and barren;

lavish garden or orchard scenes can conjure Spring fever, a Midsummer's fantasy, or the feasts of the Autumn Equinox; bare trees, mountain peaks and steely skies can feel like October or Imbolc, depending on your perspective; candlelight and woolen cloaks can run from Samhain through Yule, and on into late February snow. The elements of energetic placement can work as well—feminine imagery can be seen as the Goddess or the waxing half of the year, December through June, and masculine imagery as the God, or the waning half, Midsummer through Yule. Then, depending upon the deck, there may also be specific holiday symbolism that you can lock onto, such as Maypoles, solar wheels, harvest scythes, corn dollies, skeletons or pomegranates, evergreen wreaths, rabbits, lambs, or ornamental crosses. You know the drill—trust your instinctual eye to find whatever landmark or icon stirs you and pulls you deeper into the emotional storyline of the layout.

Some people rely on the numerology of the cards to forecast timelines, assigning the number of the card to as many days, weeks, or months, etc., for the event or situation to pan out. This method has never called to me, particularly; in fact, I've seen it used with complete inaccuracy during a reading in which, had the reader been working intuitively, they would have seen obvious signposts of the timeline that actually did transpire. Bottom line with numerology? Use it only if your instincts tell you to.

## spreads

We touched briefly on spreads at the start of chapter 5, and as promised, here are three to explore, to find out if their structure comforts or confines you. I'm going to turn you loose on these rather than walk you through with examples. The diagrams and placement outlines should give you plenty to play with.

When working with a Tarot spread, everything else stays the same—shuffling, pulling the cards, phrasing your questions, and so on. You simply lay the cards on the table in their numbered positions and interpret them one at a time within the context of their placement. You can still read the cards intuitively; you just have to intuit "inside the box" or the cross, as it were—as in our first example below.

### THE CELTIC CROSS

Perhaps the most well known and widely used of all Tarot spreads, the Celtic Cross is a layout of ten cards that "mimics" the stone crosses erected throughout Ireland on ancient sites of Pagan worship, used as a conversionary tactic by early Christian missionaries. Some find it ironic that a Tarot spread should represent the literal unseating of the Goddess religions; I find it a subtly clever thumbing-of-the-nose at the invading patriarchy. ("I'll see your cross, and raise you a High Priestess!")

Following is one version of the Celtic Cross spread; there are others to be found in which the card positions and/or meanings vary slightly. Usually this spread calls for a *significator* to be used as a focal point, either alone or in the spread itself—a card that is deliberately selected from the deck and placed to represent the querent before the reading begins, such as a Queen, to signify a mature woman, or one of the Princes for a younger man. In this version, we're skipping that practice. I think it robs the chosen card of the chance to show up later, unannounced, bearing a much more portentous message.

## celtic cross spread

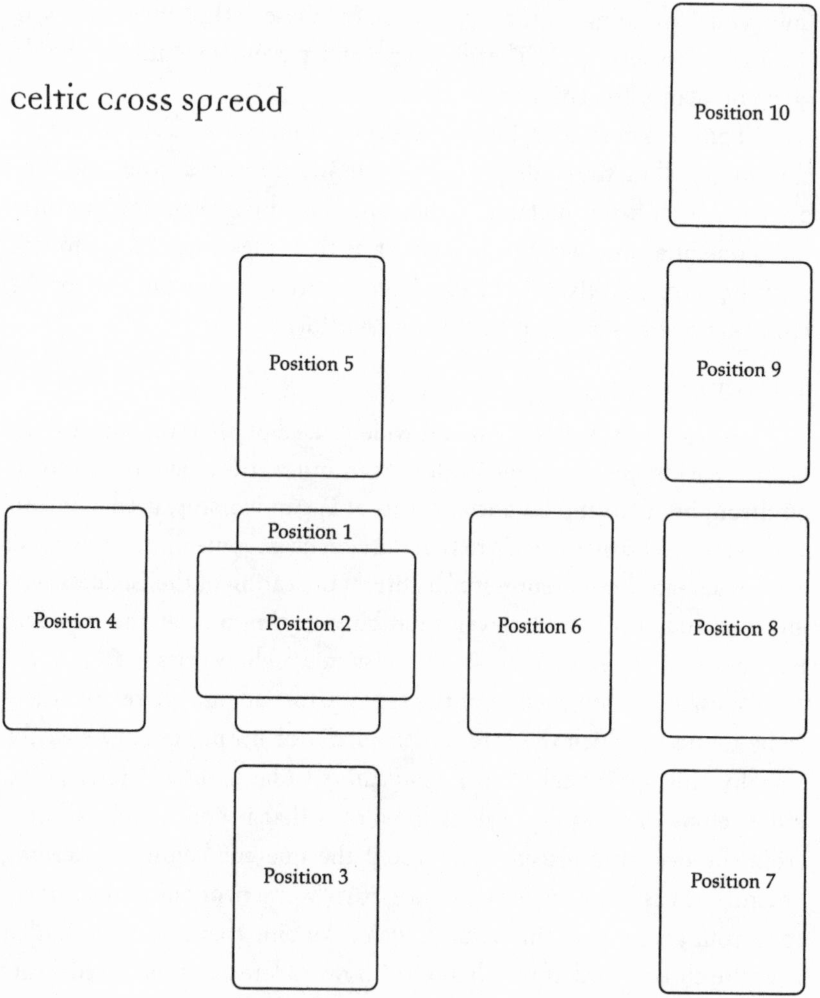

Position 10

Position 5

Position 9

Position 1

Position 4

Position 2

Position 6

Position 8

Position 3

Position 7

Position 1: *You.* This card represents the present conditions, influences, or energies affecting you or the situation at hand.

Position 2: *What crosses you.* This card represents obstacles or assistance influencing you and the situation, depending on the energy of the card.

Position 3: *What is beneath you.* This card represents the foundation of the question—past events that have determined the present conditions, memories, or long-standing behaviors that affect the situation.

Position 4: *What is behind you.* This card represents the recent past, any influence that is waning but still has some effect on the situation in question.

Position 5: *What crowns you.* This card represents a possible future, based on your energy at the moment, the goal for which to strive regarding the issue in question, and the spiritual energies that influence and assist you.

Position 6: *What lies before you.* This card represents the near future, the next step, or the short-term outcome of the situation at hand.

Position 7: *How you perceive the situation.* This card represents your attitude regarding the question and contains possible clues to thought patterns or belief structures that should be taken into consideration regarding the outcome.

Position 8: *How others see you.* This card represents how others perceive you and the support or challenge you may expect from those who have direct impact on you or the situation.

Position 9: *Your hopes and fears.* This card represents your desires and concerns for the final outcome. This is a crucial card, as it can illustrate how your thoughts and beliefs help to create your reality.

Position 10: *The final outcome.* This card represents the result of your efforts in regard to the question and indicates how the situation will likely be resolved. Look to the card in position 5 for confirmation of this end, and if there are discrepancies, it is a message that you'll have to make some different choices or take some different actions in order to achieve the outcome you desire.

## THREE-CARD SPREADS

These are sweet and simple, yet still lend themselves to interactive dynamics among the cards. You can do the Past-Present-Future spread to gain insight into the logistics of a particular situation, and then interpret the same three cards from the Mind-Body-Spirit perspective to explore the effects of that situation's outcome.

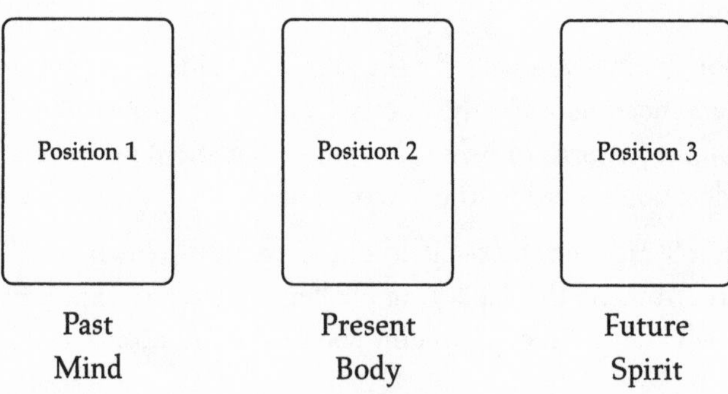

### Past-Present-Future

Position 1: This card represents past conditions, influences, or energies; pay attention to your "hit" regarding whether or not these influences are still active or if they've waned.

Position 2: This card represents the present conditions, influences, or energies.

Position 3: This card represents the possible outcome of the situation, based on the current conditions.

### Mind-Body-Spirit

Position 1: This card represents the effects of the situation on the mental level (thoughts, perceptions, awareness, attitude, judgments, etc.).

Position 2: This card represents the effects of the situation on the physical level (health, home, finances, job, environment, business, structure, etc.).

Position 3: This card represents the effects of the situation on the spiritual level (identity, passion, self-expression, karma, etc.).

As mentioned previously, I never use spreads when I'm reading for clients. But, every once in awhile, I'll mess around with one for my own stuff, either for fun or when I'm in the mood to explore, but not too deeply. This, of course, is *my* experience—if you feel more comfortable using spreads than tossing cards, if you find the specifics of the various layouts a source of focus for your psychic energies, then by all means use them. And while you're at it, make up a few of your own. (Another great use for a Tarot journal!)

## THIRTEEN

# Tarot as a Spiritual Doorway

## Using the Cards for Creativity, Ritual, and Prayer

Most people are drawn to the Tarot for one reason—to divine the future. And as a divinatory tool, the cards have no true equal. It seems a shame, however, to relegate your decks to "Oracle Only" status when the beauty and poetry of their landscapes makes for such a creative and soul-enticing ride.

I have decks all over the house; I am frequently seen carrying, shuffling, studying, fiddling. The artwork of my various acquisitions serves as a constant source of inspiration and invention; I'm pretty sure this book alone has been good for several dozen gaze-and-ponder sessions. In this chapter, I'm going to offer you ways to work with the cards outside of a psychic reading—and discover all the places you can go with a deck in your hand, even when you don't have any particular destination in mind.

## A Cosmic String around Your Finger

A life lived consciously is a magical one. Conscious living is a matter of *paying attention*—to our thoughts, words, actions, and to the signs and signals from the Universe around us. Miracles and serendipitous events become the norm when you walk in the world with that kind of awareness. One of my favorite ways to cultivate miracle consciousness is using the Tarot as a daily "reminder"—choosing one card in the morning as a focal point for the whole day.

Shuffle your deck and pull a single card, asking for guidance, focus, or for whatever your guides want you to know. Put the card somewhere you can see it as you go about your routine—on your altar, the kitchen counter, the table in the entryway where you drop your keys and sort your mail. Then watch not only for the message of the card to unfold throughout the course of your day, but also for specific images from that card to show up, quite tangibly.

One morning, years ago when I was feeling particularly challenged by life, I pulled the Six of Swords from *The Enchanted Tarot* by Amy Zerner and Monte Farber. This is a beautiful card, depicting a man and a woman in a ship on a tempestuous sea with a misty chunk of rainbow peering from out of the clouds. I gratefully intuited the ship's passage from storm to shore as an easing of my trials, at least for the day; as for the rainbow, I tucked that away as symbolic, seeing as how the sky outside my kitchen window was an unbroken stretch of September blue.

I went about my business that morning, getting snarled in hellish traffic, waiting in absurdly long lines at both post office and bank (only to reach the one teller in five who had an even gloomier outlook than mine), trying to track down a missing but much needed receipt that had apparently vaporized out of my file cabinet. Every so often the Six of Swords would pop into my head, and I was beginning to wonder if I hadn't drawn the wrong card, or at the very least missed spotting some telltale symbol hidden in the water or behind the boat, like a tidal wave or a ravenous killer shark. The storm raged on.

Finally, in the late afternoon I grabbed my gym bag and headed off to engage my frustrations in a good old-fashioned bout of free weights and treadmill tromping. As I climbed out of my car and trudged across the parking lot, I happened to look up, and in the sky overhead was a rainbow—literally, a *piece* of one, the same chunk of liquid color as on that Tarot card, sans clouds, smack dab in the center of clear open blue. If not for two fellow gym-rats coming out of the building to gawk with me, to this day I would think I had completely imagined it. It shimmered there for three or four minutes and then dissolved; we all went inside, amazed. As for the rest of my day, my own personal storms cleared pretty quickly—it's miraculous how fast your reality can change when your attitude does. Almost as miraculous as a chunk of a rainbow in a clear blue sky.

The friend with whom I had the wild Dueling Tarot experience described in chapter 12 was on hand to participate in a similarly miraculous daily-card moment. She lived an hour's drive and a fifteen minute ferry ride away; we had chatted on the phone this particular morning after getting our respective kids off to school and found we had both pulled the Ten of Hearts as our daily card. (We were getting somewhat used to this identical card gig by now; we were both using *The Enchanted Tarot* at the time as our deck of choice, and it happened *a lot.*) A few hours later I was outside puttering around in my garden when an astonishing lavender-blue butterfly came to dance around the bee balm. Astonishing, because up to that moment I had never seen a butterfly that color, and more so, because at the top of the Ten of Hearts is—you guessed it—a lavender-blue butterfly.

Just then the phone rang, and I ran in the house to get it, annoyed that someone was calling and interrupting my magical moment. I grabbed the phone and went back outside so I could keep an eye on my butterfly; I hit the button on the receiver and heard my friend's voice, breathless with excitement.

"You're never going to believe what's flying around the fuchsias on my back deck!" she said.

"The lavender-blue butterfly from the Ten of Hearts."

"Yes!" she squeaked. "How did you know?"

I laughed, in complete and utter cosmic bliss. "Because the same one's fluttering around my garden as we speak!"

The daily one-card draw puts you in direct cahoots with your guides and gives the Universe all kinds of ways to slip messages to you. Hey, life is one big classroom—you might as well pass notes and have some fun.

## Draw a Card and Cast a Spell

The Tarot is an indispensable tool for ritual and spell work, as it can heighten one's ability to visualize and emotionally connect to unformed goals and desires. "Picturing" something into being is a method of manifestation that has been used since the earliest days of our cave-dwelling ancestors; known as "sympathetic magic," employing images of the desired object or experience in order to draw it to you is an ancient and powerful form of ritual intent.

Spells and rituals using the Tarot can be as simple or as extravagant as you wish. I have danced the night away in a room aflame with candles and moonlight, around an altar draped with velvet and heaped with flowers, crystals, and twenty-one different Tarot images of the High Priestess. It took me days to come down to Earth from that one!

And I have lit a single, tiny, hand-dipped beeswax taper, studied the image of the Six of Pentacles by its flickering light, and asked Spirit to help me with a medical bill I had no way of paying. Two days later a check arrived in the mail from my insurance company for a claim I had sent in six months prior (and had all but written off because of the time lag) that was, to the dollar, the exact amount I needed to pay the bill.

Because of the transcendent nature of the imagery, the Tarot is a natural for inciting the subconscious to action and stimulating the miracle consciousness required for manifestation. In simpler terms? You have to believe it before you'll see it—and the Tarot can help you create inwardly, on the mental plane, so that what you dream of can manifest outwardly in the physical.

The trick is to choose cards that not only visually depict what you desire but also evoke the strongest emotional response to the wished-for outcome. For instance, the Ace of Pentacles for some might illustrate great wealth and security; for others, a single disk doesn't add up, so the

Nine or Ten of Pentacles is their card of choice for a money ritual.

Following are a few of my personal favorite Tarot cards for visualization and ritual intent. I use these cards because I'm so strongly drawn to and affected by their imagery. If you don't have the decks that these specific cards are from, no big deal—I'm only listing them here to use as reference, if you'd like. Remember, trust your own emotions and instincts first and choose cards from whichever deck or decks spark you the most.

*Money:* The Six and Nine of Pentacles from the *Robin Wood Tarot;* the Empress and the Queen of Pentacles from the *Hanson-Roberts Tarot;* the Sun and Fortune from the *Voyager Tarot*

*Business:* The Emperor and the Eight of Pentacles from Robin Wood; the Three and the King of Pentacles from Hanson-Roberts; the Ace of Worlds and the Eight of Crystals from Voyager

*Love:* The Two of Cups and the Four of Wands from Robin Wood; the Ace of Cups and the Lovers from Hanson-Roberts; the Six of Worlds and the Three of Cups from Voyager

*Happiness:* The Three of Cups and the Empress from Robin Wood; the Nine and Ten of Cups from Hanson-Roberts; the Ace and Nine of Cups from Voyager

*Health:* Temperance and the Star from Robin Wood; Strength and the Empress from Hanson-Roberts; the Woman of Worlds and Balance from Voyager.

*Personal Power:* The High Priestess and Judgment from Robin Wood; the Magician and Justice from Hanson-Roberts; the Woman of Wands and the Woman of Crystals from Voyager

*Creativity:* The Three of Pentacles and the Page of Cups from Robin Wood; the Sun and the Seven of Cups from Hanson-Roberts; the Child of Cups and Art from Voyager

*Spiritual Connection:* The Fool and the Hermit from Robin Wood; the Ace of Swords and the Ace of Rods from Hanson-Roberts; the Ten of Wands and the Universe from Voyager

A single card can direct your subconscious to powerful outcomes; placed in deliberate combinations, the cards and their imagery can map the story of your greatest desires. Following are three "mini" rituals you can do, using the Tarot as your point of focus and realization. You can perform these rituals as they are written, or expand on them as you like, such as burning corresponding incense, adding appropriate crystals, flowers, or other symbolic objects, working with the energies of different days or Moon cycles, and of course, casting a magic circle.[2] However you choose to do them, do them with reverence and intent, as you would any sacred act.

## An Abundance Spell

Use this spell for increasing your financial income, for meeting a particular financial obligation, or for creating a windfall.

**Supplies**

1 green candle

Powdered cinnamon

---

[2]See Michele Morgan, *Simple Wicca,* Conari Press, 2000.

1 Tarot card that represents wealth and financial abundance to you—the Six, Nine, or Ten of Pentacles; the Queen of Pentacles or the Empress if you're a woman; the King of Pentacles or the Emperor if you're a man; or any other card in your deck that invokes the energy of wealth for you

Coins and paper currency, either real or play

Lay the Tarot card face up; surround it with the coins and paper money. Place the green candle at the head of the Tarot card, and light it. Focus on the image of the card, imagining your income increasing easily and joyfully, your bank balances growing effortlessly, your bills paid in full, etc. Spend as much time on this visualization as you can, without your attention wavering. Then sprinkle small pinches of the cinnamon on the candle flame and repeat these words:

*Coins of silver, and of gold,*
*Bring me fortune, wealth untold.*
*Riches come through every door*
*To make my money ten times more.*

Continue visualizing as long as you can, sprinkling more cinnamon if you desire (the sparks are like magical little fireflies!), then proclaim the spell complete, and thank God, Goddess, or the Universe for answered prayer. Either let the candle burn out or snuff the flame and keep what remains of the candle (wrapped in one of the paper bills and tied with a green or gold cord) on your altar or somewhere sacred until your wish manifests.

## A Spell for Love

Use this spell for attracting love to you or for strengthening an existing partnership. This should go without saying, but I'm saying it anyway: *Do not* do this with an energy or intent of manipulating anyone's affections. This is a ritual for divine love, not coercion.

**Supplies**

- 2 red or pink candles
- 1 white candle
- Rose petals, fresh or dried
- Heart shaped confetti
- 1 "significator" card, representing you
- 1 "significator" card representing your current partner or the kind of partner you would like to attract
- 1 Tarot card representing true love—for example, the Ace or Two of Cups, the Four of Wands, the Lovers, etc.

Lay the significator cards side by side, leaving enough space between for a third card; set the "love" card aside for now. You may place your significator on the left or the right as you wish—if energetic placement feels right, then put the feminine to the left and the masculine to the right; if you want the two characters looking at each other, organize them accordingly; or simply trust your first instincts as to who goes where. (Someone once suggested placing the significator cards according to which side of the bed each person sleeps on. I say, whatever works!) Sprinkle the rose petals and confetti in a circle around the cards, or, if you really want to make an impression, create a heart shape. Place the red/pink candles at the head of the significator cards; place the white candle at the head of the empty space.

Light the red/pink candles. Focus on the cards and visualize yourself and your partner as two strong, independent, healthy, loving individuals, spiritually grounded, happy in your own lives, respectful of yourselves and one another, each desiring a healthy and committed partnership. Take your time with this; make it a physical and emotional realization. Then when you feel ready, place the "love" card in between, and light the white candle, speaking these words aloud:

*Lord and Lady, King and Queen,*
*Magician, Priestess, love between.*
*This bond be sacred, two in one,*
*Heart and soul 'til time is done.*

Now, visualize the kind of relationship you desire, the wonderful experiences you'll share together, the level of intimacy and connection between you, the spiritual and creative horizons you'll explore. As before, make this as real and emotionally powerful as possible and concentrate for as long as you comfortably can. Then proclaim the spell complete and give thanks for answered prayer; let the candles burn out of their own accord, or snuff the flames and keep what's left of the candles together, wrapped in a red or pink cloth with some of the rose petals, on your altar or somewhere sacred until your wish manifests.

### A Transformation Ritual

This little spell is wonderful for any circumstance with which you may be struggling—health issues, financial problems, relationship woes, etc. Healing and release may be just a candle flame away. . . .

**Supplies**

1 black candle

1 white candle

1 Tarot card representing your challenge, and 1 card representing what you would like the situation to become. Here are a few examples:

Nine of Swords/the Sun (for transforming depression, worry)

Four or Five of Pentacles/Nine of Pentacles (for financial problems)

Five of Pentacles or Ten of Swords/Strength or King of Pentacles (for health issues)

Five of Wands or Cups/Two of Cups or Four of Wands (for relationship troubles)

Eight of Swords, Five of Wands or the Tower/the Star or Temperance (for anxiety, crisis, chronic drama)

Place the black candle on the left with the "challenge" card below it, face up; the white candle on the right with the card of transformation face down. Light the black candle and focus on the image of the challenge card, thinking about your situation and its energy. Imagine channeling that energy into the candle, infusing the very wax with the problem you're facing. Then, when you're ready, speak these words aloud:

*Candle black, candle white*
*Heal this darkness with your light.*
*I now release this plight to be*
*Transformed by love so I am free.*

Now, turn the challenge card face down, deliberately; light the white candle and turn the transformation card face up. Focus on the image of this card, and this time, infuse *yourself* with the energy—of health, harmony, happiness, prosperity, whatever it is you are wishing for. Imagine the candle flames burning your challenge to cinders and charging you and your desire with vital life force. Make this visualization count; let yourself experience the healing and transformation in your mind, body, and emotions. Stay with it as long as you can; when it feels complete, proclaim the spell as such, and give thanks for answered prayer. Then either let the candles burn out (if you safely can, this is best), or snuff the flames and take what remains of the candles, bind them together with black thread, and bury them in the ground, preferably off your property.

## Om and Amen

A spell is really nothing more than a ritualized prayer, with specific actions and accoutrements that correspond to the spoken request. For those times when there's no time to do ritual or spell work, the Tarot can up the ante on your prayer power tenfold. How? Prayer is concentration; concentration is attention focused on a single object or idea. The Tarot's symbolism sparks not only the intellect but also the emotions, creating the perfect combination of inspiration and intent, all wrapped up in a neat little package.

A client of mine, new to her spiritual path, had no idea how to pray or to whom; a self-described "recovering Catholic," she had long ago given up on the conventional idea of God. She did, however, like the idea of angels, and I suggested she try using the card of Temperance as a focus for her efforts. That was five years ago, and she still "talks" to that card every morning and carries the loving and familiar image in her mind throughout the day.

I have a gorgeous fifty-year-old pine cabinet from Mexico, filled with crystals, seashells, feathers, stars, tiny lamps that burn jewel-colored oils, and many representations of the God and Goddess, some found, some purchased, some gifted to me by people I love. This is the site of years of daily prayer sessions and many an impromptu mini-ritual; when I open the scrollwork doors and light the lamps, I am immediately lifted, held, and graced by the collective energy of every wish and every gratitude ever spoken there. This is my "church," and often I will go and simply stand there, soaking in the delicious vibration, much as I imagine people sit in quiet chapels or synagogues, just hanging out at the feet of God.

Inside on the left, near a delicate silver goblet and a Ukrainian Easter egg, is the card of the High Priestess from my first copy of the *Robin Wood Tarot.* (I am currently on my sixth copy—this deck gets a lot of use in my house!) And to the right, beside a deer antler and an Aztec Sun, is the Magician, her soul mate; these two visually conjure the God and the Goddess for me, as clearly as if they'd stepped straight from the heavens to stand at my side. And when I'm in need of connection, inspiration, comfort, or support, I choose an appropriate card from the deck that resides among the crystals and seashells, and I meditate on its imagery in the lamplight, watched over by my magical guardians.

I also use the Tarot as a meditation tool with my Neuro-Linguistic Programming (NLP) clients. When someone is "blocked," unable to manifest or create positive change in their lives, nine times out of ten it's because they have no frame of reference for what they want, and therefore, no ability to visualize their desired outcome. Using the *Voyager* deck, I'll have my client go through the cards face up, choosing the images that incite the *feeling* they're going for. (This is very similar to the exercise we did in chapter 3.) Sometimes we'll play with putting their chosen cards in a particular order or pattern; other times, we'll pare the pile down to one or two of the most dramatic representations and spend awhile focusing, discussing, imagining. Then I have my client study the cards in silence for a time, meditating on the imagery, drawing the emotional energy into their bodies with every breath, claiming that energy as their own.

By the time they leave the session, my client has both a visual and an emotional link to their desired future, something I call a *barometer*—any choice that faces them, any idea that wants pursuing, can be held up to the image to see if it "fits" energetically. (Would the King of Wands choose this particular career path? If the Hierophant attended tomorrow's board meeting, how would he handle the sales presentation? Does my current relationship fit the landscape of the Three of Cups?) If so, through conscious action toward the choice or idea, coupled with prayer and continued spiritual focus, seen and unseen wheels alike are set in motion that turn dreams into absolute reality.

## Every Picture Tells a Story

One of the best extracurricular uses for the cards is igniting the creative process. I was drawn to buy my first deck because I wanted access to the imagery for story and character design; at the time, I never imagined it leading me to this particular story! (Nothing like good poetic irony.) And I still turn to the cards as a creative muse, simply studying the pictures and their elements for inspiration or actually utilizing their intuitive trigger-points as tools for plot line and character development.

A great creative exercise is to write a poem or a short story regarding a single image. Take a ride with the Prince of Pentacles through an orchard; walk awhile with the Hermit down his lantern-lit path; imagine the lives that inhabit the village seen far in the distance in the Ten of Wands. Then expand on that tale by choosing another card from the deck by sight, or challenge yourself and let the deck choose. You can also employ the Past-Present-Future spread as a Beginning-Climax-Ending guideline—again, choosing the cards by choice or by chance. Another way to play with plot development is by following the numeric energy of the cards—the cycles of growth depicted from the Ace through the Ten of the four suits (see page 81) or the journey of the Fool through the Major Arcana.

If you already have a plot in mind, use the cards to help you flesh out the personalities and histories of your different characters. Try giving your hero a specific image and then draw a card blind for the villain; or let your champion be the mystery man and your Judas come from chosen stock. What happens when the aristocratic matriarch in the Ten of Pentacles hires the charismatic soldier-of-arms in the Five of Swords? Lock up your maidens in the Three of Cups—there's intrigue afoot, I tell you! And don't worry that you'll be limited to medieval allegory. (Think Shakespeare, à la *West Side Story.*) The timeless quality of the Tarot's symbolism makes for ageless storytelling.

Writing isn't the only art form inspired by the Tarot. You can dance the scene from the Five of Wands; sing in the Queen of Swords' sultry voice; act an impromptu vignette between the maiden of Strength and Death's enigmatic reaper. Collage is a natural expression of the Tarot's layered influences, as is any medium involving color and movement. Create your own Tarot deck, card by card—start with just the Major Arcana, if an entire deck seems a daunting proposal, and you can still have fun doing readings with the finished twenty-two trumps while you move on to the pips. Climb inside your favorite card and look around, then come home and find your favorite way to share or record your experience. The Tarot is a peerless champion not only to the intuition but also the imagination, and to your own creative genius.

## FOURTEEN

# "So Whaddya Think I Am, Some Kind of Mind Reader?"

## Finding a Psychic You Can Trust

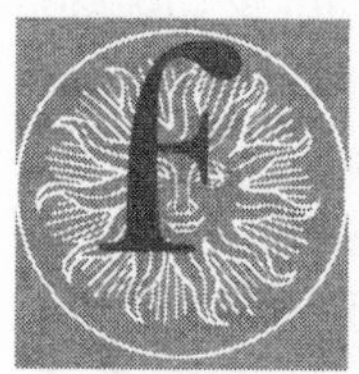

Firelight glints against a gilt-stitched canopy; overhead, the moon is a slender silver cusp in the evening sky, a single star held captive in its icy curve. Faces ring the fire, handsome and wild, laughing, sharing thin brown paper cigarettes and a jug of bitter wine. Children play hide-and-seek in the smoke and flickering shadows, while beneath the canopy sits a woman, veiled in dark lace and lamplight, jeweled rings glittering on every finger, a deck of battered cards in her hands.

Somewhere in the distant hills, wolves begin a lament of night and sorrow; the ponies hobbled near the clapboard wagons shiver and snort, their harnesses jingling, as a stranger enters the camp, moves through the fire-lit gathering, steps beneath the canopy where the woman waits. A handful of silver coins is spilled across the table; a match is struck, and a bargain with it; the woman's eyes are dark, as deep as the night sky beyond the camp fire, filled with magic and the knowledge of mysterious and wondrous things. The stranger sits waiting, poised between fear and desire, the future and his fate spilled on the table like a scattering of silver. And as the candles are lit and the cards are turned, in a single moment, the path is revealed. . . .

So what's it like, being a modern-day mystic? For the most part, there are no caravans or campfires, no wolves howling in the moonlit distance. But the mystery and wonder are still very much alive for me, as is the sense of anticipation, and yes, sometimes even fear, on the part of everyone who sits down across from me at my card-strewn table.

My job as a psychic is to offer my clients a "blueprint" of the future based on the energy and focus of the present moment. Having this kind of map allows you to embrace the opportunities and meet the challenges of life head-on, prepared to maximize the potential of every experience. For those who've never experienced a psychic reading, the idea of glimpsing the future can be frightening indeed, especially if they think their fate has long been sealed by some omnipotent, dispassionate God.

The truth is, the future is like quicksilver—it flows toward and shapes itself to whatever form you offer it. And a psychic reading lets you test that flow in advance, empowering you to work your own God-given magic ahead of time to determine final outcomes. If you like what you see in a reading, you can avail yourself of the predicted events either by taking action toward them or by hanging out and allowing events to unfold toward you. If you don't like what you see, you can change your direction and thus change your future.

In this chapter, I'm going to address some of the more frequently asked questions regarding psychic readings, for the purpose of educating those of you seeking a professional reader and those of you perhaps wanting to become one. Please bear in mind these answers are from my perspective and in my opinion only—you'll find plenty, I'm sure, who would contest what I have to say. But hey, that's what makes life interesting and keeps the faeries busy in the woods. So take what you like and leave the rest and, as always, keep your own instincts at the top of the totem pole.

## What should I expect from a psychic reading?

A psychic reading, above all else, should leave you feeling empowered. You should walk away with a renewed sense of confidence, hope, peace, and more than a few tools tucked into your belt with which to design and construct your destiny.

The best psychic readings serve to confirm what you already instinctively know, helping to validate your intuitive sense of things and clarify the path (or paths) that already lie before you. For that, expect the information you receive to "ring true" on some level, even if a part of you doesn't really want to hear it. In the most basic sense, nothing a psychic says should surprise you. Instead, expect to be energized, excited, and brought back to center all at the same time—just like any other true spiritual experience.

When someone comes to me for a reading, I believe it is my

spiritual and ethical duty to send them out into the world an hour later armed with the knowledge of their highest potential and as much awareness and insight to reach that potential as I can give them. The challenges that appear on the horizon are marked as learning opportunities rather than predicaments; the rewards that glitter and spark in the distance are recognized, acknowledged, and appreciated in advance, setting energies in motion to call them home. The warrior-soul is tapped, and the spirit is aligned with its human counterpart—and my job is complete when my client walks out the door knowing they are truly the master of their destiny and more than equal to anything life may hand them.

**Should psychics be paid for doing readings?**

There are two very separate camps regarding this issue. I have heard the philosophy that a "true" psychic would never charge money for a reading, as it is a spiritual art and should never be tainted with worldly energy. Having the utmost respect for religious and spiritual viewpoints, I say to each his own when it comes to belief systems.

I, however, stand in the second camp regarding spirituality and money. My philosophy? Money is Divine energy, and a psychic reading is an energy exchange. Psychics have real lives, with real bills to pay—if I didn't charge for my readings, I would have to have another career to support myself and my family, and I wouldn't have the time or the energy to help all the people I do now. I look upon the spiritual work that I do as no different from the work of a doctor, therapist, minister, or any other healer—and I find that people are more likely to take a psychic reading seriously and use the information to their greatest advantage if they invest something in it first.

I've known psychics who charged outrageous sums of money for a session, and I've known those who earned pennies for their services. Fees vary, as do readers, and you don't always get what you pay for, so again, trust your instincts from the start. The best psychics have a strong rep, a loyal following, and their fees reflect well on their abilities.

## How can I tell if someone is a "good" psychic?

At the risk of dealing in judgments, I think this is an important question, and I frequently address this very issue in classes and lectures. Working with a psychic is really no different from working with a doctor or a counselor; it's crucial to choose someone with a reputation for integrity and honesty. Word of mouth is the best barometer of a reader's character and abilities.

First and foremost, you should feel a comfortable connection with the reader, almost a familiarity, pretty much from the moment you meet them. When someone is truly tapped in to you psychically, they are vibrating to your frequency, so to speak, and rapport will come naturally as a result. This is why trusting your own intuition is even more important that trusting the reader's. Some nervousness at the beginning is perfectly natural; I still get a little buzz just before I have a reading done for me by someone new, but there's quite a difference between anticipation and unease. Remember the exercise in chapter 3, regarding "good" cards and "bad" cards? Same gig. If a reader puts you off energetically, pay attention. At the very least, it's going to be tough to get a credible reading from someone you're not comfortable with, and in extreme cases, that discomfort is trying to save you from an experience that can wreak potential emotional havoc on your psychic landscape.

A year or so ago a sweet, shy little woman came to see me, sent by a friend who was already one of my clients. When she walked into my office, this woman was literally trembling with fear. A tearful story revealed that the previous week she had gone to another Tarot reader, drawn by a sandwich board on the side of the road advertising Psychic and Spiritual Guidance, to seek insight into an unhappy job situation and some family issues. The "psychic and spiritual guidance" this woman received was to be told that she was under an extremely dark curse, complete with a detailed list of *horrific* events that would befall her and everyone she cared about unless she immediately paid $700 to have said curse removed.

Unfortunately, this so-called psychic was plugged in just enough; she fleshed out the curse's projected effects with enough information regarding its intended victims to make her story sound credible to my by-then terrified client. This woman told me she actually had her checkbook in hand, pen poised to retain the psychic's life-saving services, when something inside of her screamed to get the *#@&!* out of there. (The faeries by that time had most likely chucked flitting in and out of the forest to get her attention and had advanced straight to the stage of setting fire to the trees.) My client managed to escape the reading with her bank account intact, but not without her nerves and her faith desperately and unequivocally violated.

*If* I believed in Hell, I would also believe that there is an especially toasty corner there reserved for people in positions of spiritual and emotional authority who use their talents and abilities to exploit others. Obviously, the above example is an extreme one; not all bad experiences come with fraud attached. Some readers are just intensely negative; delivering everything that comes up in a reading with undue criticism, personal projection, or an unabashed air of impending doom. And my absolute advice in any of these situations is this: Get up and walk out. No matter what. I would rather see you err on the side of paranoia than subject your psyche to the aftermath of an adverse psychic experience.

I've spent a fair portion of my career doing damage control for people who've either had the bejeezus scared out of them or been left feeling hopelessly depressed by a negative or insensitive reader. This is not to say that a reading should only be hearts and flowers, but a good psychic is compassionate, clear, and has an ability to present all of the information they receive in the most empowering way possible for their clients, both the good and the bad. (More information on "Bad News" coming up.) Life can be complicated; it doesn't have to be terrifying. What's that saying? Challenge is inevitable, but struggle is an option? *That* is God talking, and the best psychics deliver Divine information in a context that acknowledges and advocates their client's free will, conscious choice, and God-directed ability to change the shape of their destiny.

Once again, *trust your own instincts* about any reader whose services you retain. The really questionable ones are usually just that—really questionable. If it's that you simply don't feel comfortable, pay attention—you'll have to be the judge of whether your discomfort is based upon rapport (or lack of) between you and the reader, or whether it is because you might not want to hear a truth you already ultimately know.

### How much information should I give the reader?

The rapport between client and reader is a two-way street, most definitely, and cannot solely be the reader's responsibility. When someone sits down at my table, I absolutely ask questions—to engage their energy and to give me a language with which to communicate the information that comes in. I usually ask what astrological sign they are and their age to begin with; then, as the reading progresses, I might ask a few questions regarding the hits I'm receiving, to allow myself a clearer means of presentation.

Every so often I've encountered someone who comes in for a session, sits down across from me, and due to either fear or cynicism (same thing, slightly different expression) they might as well be shut inside a bank vault, doors slammed tight and bolted with that big wheel-thingie that looks like it belongs on a submarine hatch. *Boom.* Nary a whisper of energy escapes them; even their body language screams, "No *way* are you gettin' in here!" I've even had a few instances where my standard break-the-ice question ("So, what are we looking at for you today?") is immediately fielded and volleyed back with, "You're the psychic. You tell *me.*"

Sigh. I call this "TTRS," or "Test-the-Reader Syndrome." Thank the gods this is a relatively rare phenomenon. But if and when it happens, here's my generic response to three-foot-thick, bullet- and waterproof steel:

A true psychic reading cannot be "influenced." The psychic information received by the reader is based on seeds of action and energy that have already taken root in the present. In other words, what you already know, already *is;* what you don't know, and what brought you (presumably) to the reading in the first place, is the potential unfolding of your current reality, based on the present energy. Therefore, the more open you are with a reader, the more open the channels of info they can receive on your behalf. By clamming up and shutting down energetically, you waste your time, as well as the reader's abilities, in a sticky little game called That's for Me to Know, And You to Find Out.

Some people feel the need to be "impressed" by a psychic's abilities before they can relax and participate in the process. Going to a psychic reader should be less about parlor tricks and more about creating a sacred connection that benefits you both emotionally and spiritually. As far as being impressed goes, don't worry—I guarantee you'll be *amazed,* given the magical nature of Universal Wisdom and the Tarot's inimitable delivery. But you'll be much more impressed with what a reader can uncover for you if you'll open up and give a little at the start.

Now, since we're swinging the pendulum from every angle here, the *downside* to opening up is the client who spends forty-five minutes out of an hour telling me their entire life history, and I get to cram an hour's worth of info into the remaining fifteen. Or, the reader who asks a million leading questions, divining their client's future by process of elimination rather than intuition. Rapport and connection is a natural phenomenon marked by comfort, both emotional and physical, facilitated by a willingness to be open, both energetically and expressively, and supported by that all-important magical ingredient known as *trust*. Broken-Record Syndrome aside, trusting your own instincts as to how much you share will help create the perfect balance of give and take between you and your chosen psychic.

### What about accuracy?

The accuracy of a reading depends upon two factors: how in sync the reader is with the seeker, and what the seeker ultimately chooses to do with the information he or she receives. The sync thing we've already covered; free will and conscious choice are always a deciding factor in how a probable future plays out.

Generally speaking, you can expect the best psychics to be approximately 70 percent to 90 percent accurate. Remember the psychic energy cycles we talked about in chapter 5? Those fluctuations can have bearing on any psychic reading, regardless of whether or not the reader is a professional. It's been my experience, however, that while those cycles are much more pronounced when I'm reading the cards for myself, when I'm plugging in for someone else, I can circumvent the energetic obstacles almost completely. I think it's because of my attitude regarding the work that I do—when I'm with a client, I'm acting as chief translator in a crucial meeting of the minds between the seeker and God. It's my job to be clear.

Given that a psychic reading shows only the potential future, it's essential to remember that there are always variables in any situation, and the state of the planet in the New Millennium/Aquarian Age is all about flow and flexibility, acceleration of time and energy, and assuming personal responsibility for one's reality. People used to be able to get away with a serious amount of unconsciousness and still keep their lives at status quo; John Lennon was indeed a prophet when he proclaimed "Instant Karma," because the future turns on a dime these days as a result of both conscious and unconscious choice.

Over the years, I've had to curb the desire to follow clients home and make sure they stick to the cosmic path that shows up for them in a reading. But my job is to merely impart information, and what my client does with that information when they walk out the door is entirely up to them. Either they take to heart, and thus to action, the guidance and consciousness given to them through the cards, or they completely ignore it and let the future unfold in its own inimitable and sometimes fractious way. Either way, I inevitably get to say, "I told you so," which my righteous Sagittarian nature absolutely *loves.* But believe me, I have a lot more fun saying it with a smile on my face as opposed to a grimace.

### What about "bad" news?

Because my purpose in a psychic reading is to show my clients the high road, so to speak, I've had people question whether their reading was legitimate because I wasn't telling them anything "bad." I respond by offering to go through my deck and find the darkest, scariest looking cards I can find and expound on them at length if it would make them feel any better. So far, no one's taken me up on it.

It isn't that I don't relay challenging news—whatever comes through, I pass on. In fact, it's impossible for me *not* to relay what I receive, because, as much as I dislike the buzzword, I'm channeling.

But as I've said before, I approach cards of challenge as opportunities for growth and change, as opposed to portents of inexorable doom, and I present every shred of information regarding those growth opportunities accordingly. This doesn't mean I sugarcoat anything. Rather, my proposal is this: Here's the garbage; you have two choices. You can be the victim, or you can be the warrior. Loss, sorrow, disappointment, heartache—all are part and parcel of the human experience. It isn't what happens, but rather, what we do with what happens, that truly determines our destinies—and as far as I'm concerned, *that* kind of insight is the entire purpose of a psychic reading.

There are times, though rare, when a pivotal event is *not* foreseen in a reading and comes to pass anyway, with life-changing results. Once a couple came to me seeking insight into planning a pregnancy; they had suffered two miscarriages already and were extremely skittish about trying again. I tapped in to the gender and energetic personality of the child that was coming, gave them a timeline for the conception, and saw the pregnancy and birth going smoothly. Sure enough, things went along happily right on schedule until the end of the first trimester when they had another miscarriage. We were all devastated—nothing even remotely suggesting loss had come up in the reading. But as a result of this third experience, they consulted a specialist who discovered a "hidden" health issue in the woman that, left undiscovered, would have caused repeated failed pregnancies *and* become a major complication later on in her life. Not only was the health problem addressed, but the couple also turned to counseling to deal with the emotional aftermath of the experience, and in the process, resolved long-standing communication and intimacy issues between them, thus dramatically strengthening their relationship. A year later, they became pregnant again and went on to have their miracle baby, exactly as originally foretold.

Later on, I had occasion to ask the couple what they would have done if we had indeed foreseen another miscarriage. They told me without question they would have turned to adoption to have a child, and as a result would not have addressed the health or relationship issues until they presented themselves in potentially lethal guise later on.

The information received in a psychic reading is for the purpose of conscious growth and empowerment. If you are forewarned of something in a reading, it is because you are meant to shift the face of your future through action and awareness. Then there are those lessons that apparently cannot be learned unless we come to the train track completely blind and get run over by them. At times it seems we signed a contract somewhere stating that as human beings things have to get *really* uncomfortable before we'll change. But the truth is, the more conscious you become, the easier the lessons; and a psychic reading is a phenomenal tool for avoiding Cosmic Freight Trains.

I've also had to apologize to a few clients in my career for the fact that I was not going to tell them what they wanted to hear. Some people come to a reading demanding to know when their abusive or emotionally unavailable partner is going to turn into Prince or Princess Charming, sans counseling, or when their own financial woes will morph into unlimited abundance, despite an overwhelming attitude of lack. They want answers, solutions, absolutes; I give them options, awareness, and homework. Not everyone wants to be responsible for his or her own reality, but I feel that is the sole (and the *soul)* reason for the work that I do—to impart to my fellow beings the power to transform themselves and their lives.

## The Rewards

I have been asked a number of times over the years how I handle the pressure of imparting life-altering information to people. For me, it has never been anything other than a passion and a delight. My clients are like my kids—I laugh with them, cry with them, applaud their endeavors, help steer them through inevitable storms, and constantly remind myself that *everyone is ultimately responsible for creating their own reality.* I have no words to describe the sense of satisfaction and joy I feel watching my "family" learn, grow, and achieve their dreams, and how honored I am to be part of the journey.

I've had the singular pleasure of dancing at the weddings of couples whom I "introduced" psychically, long before they actually met; been invited to houses that I described in detail for their prospective owners; and held babies whom I encountered in the womb, or before—including my proudest psychic "birth," that of my godson Jake (who not only showed up with the exact astrological and personality traits I divined years before his debut, but who was kind enough to give me, in advance, the precise *minute* he would arrive. Thanks, kiddo!).

I've tapped in to past lives that were so real I physically felt the experience—opening a door for the release of an energy that had held someone back for countless lifetimes. I've helped create closure in the loss of loved ones, dialoguing with both people and pets who've crossed over—allowing the living to move on to peace and healing. I've introduced clients to their spirit guides, the angelic presences that protect and champion all of us but who often remain a mystery until someone gives them a face and a name. I get to be that someone, and it never ceases to completely amaze and absolutely humble me. And above all else, I get to be a conduit for God, a liaison between a human who is searching and a spirit who has never left home—and my own life is changed and blessed on a daily basis because of it.

FIFTEEN

# Attitude, Intent, and the Cosmic Telephone

## Final Thoughts

*We shall not cease from exploration, and*
*the end of all our exploring will be to arrive where we*
*started and know the place for the first time.*

—T. S. Eliot

On a frost-silvered night in late January, a lifetime ago, it seems, my world was forever, unequivocally changed. As I left the Tarot class at Stargazers, I remember the Moon hanging low over the light-strewn valley that lay between my house and town; She was full, wearing a smoky ring of faerie-fire and an expression of deep satisfaction on Her beautiful, mystical face. To this day, I'm convinced the tires of my car never touched the road, and that drive home was the beginning of a remarkable journey, one that stretches on with infinite possibility across a magical and enduring horizon.

Through the window of the Tarot, I have witnessed over and over the best in myself and others, been offered the chance to sidestep shadows and heartache, and been handed the map to lands beyond the limited vision of my human experience. The cards and their stories have challenged me, comforted me, become part of my bones and my soul; their images still captivate, as beautiful and as mysterious as the first time I saw them.

For some, Tarot cards are the Devil's handiwork, evil in disguise as pretty pictures. That subject is a whole other book, entirely. Others see the cards as pure entertainment, the fine print in a 1-900 advertisement. (Skeptics are a favorite pastime of mine—I've yet to meet one I couldn't convert.) For me, the cards are a gift from Spirit, a direct line to the collective consciousness, a remarkable, inspired, hands-on tool for sacred connection. They are not, however, where the answers come from.

When you call someone on the telephone, I hope you don't convince yourself that the phone is the one speaking to you. Tarot cards are essentially the same kind of instrument—a channel for Divine information, not the source. It can be surprisingly easy to forget who's in charge.

When I first began working with the cards, I had occasion to learn just how willing my human self was to surrender my power and instinct to something outside of myself. It began quietly enough, I suppose, as nothing more than awe for the magical nature of the cards and their messages. Time and again I was completely amazed by the indisputable clarity of the images I pulled, the perfectly corresponding symbolisms, the mind-boggling accuracy of their aim. Somewhere, however, a line got crossed, and suddenly it was no longer my intuition doing the talking. I remember feeling it, almost physically, this sensation of being outside of my own skin, looking at the cards as if they alone contained every magic and every answer. At that point, I shut the door tightly on God and guidance, hanging out in this strange, disjointed reality, until finally someone upstairs got wise to me and pushed my deck to spew a particularly dark and frightening layout regarding someone I cared about a great deal, complete with seemingly precise intuitive hits. Talk about portents of impending doom.

I, of course, completely freaked. I called a dear and trusted spiritual mentor, who immediately told me to put my deck down and not pick it up again for three days, and to spend that three days in prayer and meditation asking for clarity on what I had seen. By mid-morning, day 3, I felt the door creak open, and light once again flooded my lopsided world; I realized with startling simplicity that those dark cards had instead been divining *my* future—this three-day nightmare of my own making, the very experience I was just now climbing my way up and out of. (Nothing even remotely negative happened to the person I believed the reading was for.) I was left humbled, relieved, more than a bit sheepish, but thankfully back in my own skin, light-years wiser in the ways of magic and oracles, and in the understanding that unless you listen to the voice inside yourself first, you'll never be able to hear God in anything or anyone else.

Your cards and this book are merely tools to help you access psychic information. Don't give your power away to them or to any other spiritual object. I don't believe God wants us to give our power away even to Him—but rather, to join forces with Him to co-create a Divine reality.

Spiritual tools have no true magic other than that with which we entreat them. But as humans, because our emotional selves are so closely tied to our physical senses, it is essential to have something tangible, something to touch and see and experience, that can help us hold the space for God. Used with reverence, love, and sacred intent, the Tarot is an invaluable medium for creating such a space, for connecting with the intuitive nature, and helping to find the balance between your human self and your spirit. But always remember that yours is the truest voice . . . and you already know all the answers.

# ACKNOWLEDGMENTS

This book proved quite a journey for me . . . as life within the creative process usually is. My heartfelt thanks to the following bright souls, who traveled with me all the way:

Tess Sterling—for meeting me at the first door and opening many others after, without knowing it.

Suki and Karen—for nights of impossible laughter and magical possibilities . . . and to Robin C., who was there for the very beginning.

Leslie Berriman—my editor, for unswerving belief in this project, and in me; for giving my voice free rein, and for bringing out the best in my writing.

Everyone at Conari Press, for the warmest welcome, and the happiest home.

My family—Mom and Dad, for faith and unfailing support (and special thanks to Dad, for channeling the voice of God when I couldn't hear Him anywhere else); Mitch, April, Chelsea, and Shayne, for Texas hospitality and unending love, long-distance. I love you all.

Kim Schneider. Here we are, volume 2—and your abiding belief in me and the strength of our friendship continues to comfort and amaze me. Now it's your turn, Missy . . . and I've got my pompoms at the ready.

Gary, Sami, and Jake Schneider—for sharing Kim with me, and letting me be part of your family.

Nan Yurkanis—for kaleidoscopes of all kinds, and for the joy and ease of a friendship without rules, and without limitation ... and to Jonathan Yurkanis, for simplicity, grace, and the power of words.

Rebecca Richards—for a connection that continues to evolve, both personally and professionally, and for a path shared, straight toward heaven. You are such a gift!

Marcus Henschell—for honesty, integrity, and that irrepressible Scorpio charm.

All my students and clients— for being my greatest teachers.

To my daughter, Kaeleigh—for growing into one of the most amazing women I have ever had the pleasure to know. You crack my heart, and soothe my soul ... and bring me more joy than I have words for. (And you, of all people, should know that's no small feat.) I love you, Bink.

And to Richard GreyEagle—for being proof positive that angels do indeed come to Earth in human form ... and that not only does God exist, He pays attention.

# SUGGESTED READING

Following are a few of the books that have helped me over the years in my explorations of the Tarot:

Arrien, Angeles. *The Tarot Handbook.* Sonoma, CA: Arcus Publishing Company, 1987. This book contains some amazing information regarding psychology, cultural anthropology, and archetypal symbolism in the Tarot. Great numerological and astrological correspondences for each card as well.

Echols, Signe E., Robert Mueller, and Sandra A. Thomson. *Spiritual Tarot.* New York: Avon Books, 1996. I love the way the interpretations of the cards are handled— written as though the cards were actually speaking.

Renee, Janina. *Tarot Spells.* St. Paul: Llewellyn Publications, 1990. This is such a wonderful resource for using the Tarot in ritual and spell work. Specific spells for everything you can think of and then some.

Shavick, Nancy. *The Tarot Reader.* New York: Berkley Publishing, 1991. I love this quirky little book— the interpretations for each card cover every possible topic in a reading, such as love, work, health, etc. And the whole book is hand-printed!

Zerner, Amy, and Monte Farber. *The Enchanted Tarot* (book and card set). St. Martin's Press, 1990. The book that accompanies *The Enchanted Tarot* is as exquisite as the deck— along with the interpretations, the book contains full-color reproductions of each card and a little spell or ritual that corresponds to the cards' energy. Just watch out if the boxed set is on a shelf above you!

# INDEX

## J



## K



## L



## M



## N



## P

## ABOUT THE AUTHOR

Michele Morgan has been a professional psychic, Tarot counselor, certified NLP practitioner, teacher, and writer for over a decade. She conducts private sessions as well as classes and workshops from her sanctuary in Snohomish, Washington, called RavenHeart, A Center for Spirit and Healing. In addition to writing monthly psychic insights on her popular Web site, Michele is the author of *Simple Wicca* (Conari Press, 2000). She lives in a magical house in Snohomish with her daughter, their dog, three cats, a rabbit, and a tame deer named Flower. You can contact Michele at her Web site at *www.heartoftheraven.com.*

# TO OUR READERS

Conari Press publishes books on topics ranging from spirituality, personal growth, and relationships to women's issues, parenting, and social issues. Our mission is to publish quality books that will make a difference in people's lives—how we feel about ourselves and how we relate to one another. We value integrity, compassion, and receptivity, both in the books we publish and in the way we do business.

As a member of the community, we donate our damaged books to nonprofit organizations, dedicate a portion of our proceeds from certain books to charitable causes, and continually look for new ways to use natural resources as wisely as possible.

Our readers are our most important resource, and we value your input, suggestions, and ideas about what you would like to see published. Please feel free to contact us, to request our latest book catalog, or to be added to our mailing list.

2550 Ninth Street, Suite 101
Berkeley, California 94710-2551
800-685-9595 • 510-649-7175
fax: 510-649-7190 • e-mail: conari@conari.com
www.conari.com